camps

RETREATS, MISSIONS, & SERVICE IDEAS

FOR YOUTH GROUPS

THE *ideas* LIBRARY

THE IDEAS LIBRARY

camps RETREATS, MISSIONS, & SERVICE IDEAS

THE ideas LIBRARY

FOR YOUTH GROUPS

Youth Specialties

ZondervanPublishingHouse
Grand Rapids, Michigan
A Division of HarperCollins*Publishers*

Camps, Retreats, Missions, & Service Ideas
Copyright © 1997 by Youth Specialties, Inc.
Youth Specialties Books, 1224 Greenfield Dr., El Cajon, CA 92021, are published by Zondervan Publishing House, 5300 Patterson Ave. S.E., Grand Rapids, MI 49530.

Ideas in this book have been voluntarily submitted by individuals and groups who claim to have used them in one form or another with their youth groups. Before you use an idea, evaluate it for its suitability to your own group, for any potential risks, for safety precautions that must be taken, and for advance preparation that may be required. Youth Specialties, Inc., and Zondervan Publishing House are not responsible for, nor have any control over, the use or misuse of any of the ideas published in this book.

Project editor: Vicki Newby
Cover and interior design: Curt Sell
Art director: Mark Rayburn
ISBN: 0-310-22032-7

Printed in the United States of America

98 99 00 01 02 03 04 05 06/ /10 9 8 7 6 5 4 3

CONTENTS

So what killer idea have you invented lately?

Are your kids still talking about that activity you invented for your last retreat or missions trip? Youth Specialties pays $25 (and in some cases, more) for unpublished, field-tested ideas that have worked for you.

You've probably been in youth work long enough to realize that sanitary, theoretical, tidy ideas aren't what in-the-trenches youth workers are looking for. They want—you want—imagination and take-'em-by-surprise novelty for retreats and other events. Ideas that have been tested and tempered and improved in the very real, very adolescent world you work in.

So here's what to do:

• Sit down at your computer, get your killer idea out of your head and onto your hard drive, then e-mail it to ideas@youthspecialties.com. Or print it off and fax it to 619-440-4939 (Attn: Ideas).

• If you need to include diagrams, photos, art, or samples that help explain your idea, stick it all in an envelope and mail it to our street address: Ideas, 1224 Greenfield Dr., El Cajon, CA 92021-3399.

• Be sure to include your name and all your addresses and numbers.

Let us have about three months to give your idea a thumbs up or down*, and a little longer for your 25 bucks.

*Hey, no offense intended if your idea isn't accepted. It's just that our fussy Ideas Library editor has these *really* meticulous standards. If the idea isn't creative, original, and just plain fun in an utterly wild or delightful way, she'll reject it (reluctantly, though, because she has a tender heart). Sorry. But we figure you deserve only the best ideas.

CAMPS AND RETREATS

Organizing successful camp and retreats is one of the more complex and time-consuming tasks a youth leader faces. It can also be one of the most life-changing experiences your students can have during their adolescence. No matter what kind of camp or retreat you're planning, you'll find vital information here to help you.

LEADERSHIP

BASIC PRINCIPLES OF RUNNING CAMPS AND RETREATS

Most churches have some kind of camping program, but many churches do not have a consistent, well-thought-out camping philosophy.

It is obvious that at some point your youth group ought to formulate a camping philosophy notebook which can be used indefinitely for whoever is responsible for the camping program. To help you with that formulation, we have attempted to provide you with a summary of the most effective camping information available.

• **People-Program-Facility.** That is the fundamental order of priorities for any camping philosophy. For some, the facilities are most important. But fancy cabins with carpeting and drapes cannot compensate for poor leadership and shabby programming. Many churches meet at campgrounds where the

camp director is also the director of maintenance. Too often this results in a program that serves the facility. The kids get lectured for scuffing the floor or a game gets canceled because it might dirty the meeting hall, etc. The most important aspect of any camping program is the leadership personnel. Poor, even inadequate facilities can be compensated for if the program and personnel are tops.

• **Food.** Good food does not mean expensive food. Spaghetti is fine as long as it is not overcooked. Hot dogs and sloppy joes are great as long as they are not soggy. If the food is poor, the kids will never forget it. Not only must you have good quality food, but you must have plenty of food so that the kids feel free to go back for seconds and thirds.

• **Results.** Many decisions are made at camps and conferences. But for many churches the only justification of the camping program is the number of decisions made at camp. It is more important to be concerned with the process of contemplation that occurs at camp rather than the results, meaning overt public response to a message or messages. Camp is a time for self-evaluation away from the

13

rut of the teenage environment. It is a time for new thoughts and new experiences. Kids are able to concentrate their thinking while hearing the message in concentrated form.

It's not unusual to hear young people talk about their decision made at a conference and subsequent failure to live up to it. It is so important to prepare campers for the inevitable "honeymoon's over" feeling. Prepare them for the sobering reality of going home where everything is exactly the way they left it. Be careful that you do not communicate to kids that the entire value of their time at camp is determined by their positive response to the call for commitment.

• **Post-Camp.** After each conference, consider having the campers take over one of the church services. Include a camp choir (made up of all the campers), testimonies, report on camp, and, if possible, a short talk by the camp speaker. (Encourage the speaker to relate his or her remarks to what was said at camp.) A general report to the church accomplishes a number of important goals: First of all, those who did not attend will get a feeling for the spiritual progress made at camp. Secondly, those parents who have just heard about the worst things at camp (kids always tell their parents the worst) will get a more complete view of the conference by hearing the positive and constructive side. Another suggestion is to have a camp reunion about a month or so after camp, where camp movies are shown along with refreshments and a short follow-up message by the camp speaker. This is an excellent way to keep contact with those who attended camp but for some reason haven't kept in touch with the church or youth group.

CAMP SURVEY

The survey on page 15 was used at a large high school camp to feel the pulse of the kids. It was a great help to the camp leaders and speakers in determining just what direction to move in.

PERSONAL GOAL SETTING

Before your group leaves for a retreat, give personal goals charts on page 16 to group members. Encourage teens to list their goals for the retreat in the right-hand column. They may want to include goals such as making new friends, controlling their temper, or growing closer to God. They can share their goals with one other person if they like. During the retreat, give your teens time each night to fill in their charts using the symbols found beneath it. At the end of the week, discuss whether or not goals were reached and why. *Ben Sharpton.*

CAMPING SCHEDULES

Believe it or not, the schedule of a camp is one of the prime factors affecting the outcome of the conference. If the schedule is too structured, the campers will complain and rebel; but if the schedule is too unstructured, then the campers will be bored and complain that there is nothing to do. The following schedules are representative schedules from some of the most effective camping programs in the country:

• **Weekend Camp**
  Friday
  6:00 Dinner
  7:30 Evening meeting
  9:00 Special activity
  11:00 Lights out
  Saturday
  7:00 Wake up
  8:30 Breakfast
  11:30 Discussions, small groups, lecture
  12:30 Lunch
  1:30 Free time
  4:30 Elective
  6:00 Dinner
  7:30 Evening meeting
  11:00 Lights out
  Sunday
  7:00 Wake up
  8:30 Breakfast
  11:30 Morning meeting
  12:30 Lunch
  1:30 Head for home

Junior high may require a slightly earlier lights-out time. College age can go to bed when they want to.

• **Weekly Camp**
  7:00 Wake up
  8:00 Breakfast

Tell it like it is!

Answer each question briefly and honestly. Say what you really believe. Do not put your name anywhere on this sheet.

1. I am _____ years old.

2. I am a (boy)_____(girl)_____.

3. I am a Christian. (yes)_____(no)_____

4. I have _____ parents who are Christians.
$\quad\quad\quad$ (number)

5. A Christian is a person who _____.

6. I go to church (or don't go to church) because_____

_____.

7. My friends go to church (or don't go to church) because _____

_____.

8. I came to this camp because _____.

9. My biggest gripe about church is _____.

10. My biggest gripe about camps is _____.

11. My biggest gripe about parents (adults) is _____

_____.

12. I wish that _____.

My Goals Chart

In the column on the right, list all of your goals for the upcoming retreat (make new friends, grow closer to God, etc.). Then share these goals with a partner. Each evening during the retreat, take time to update your chart and create new goals using the symbols presented at the bottom of this chart. At the end of the week, tell your partner about your goal-setting experience.

Goals	Sunday	Monday	Tuesday	Wednesday	Thursday	Friday

MOUNTAIN-TOP EXPERIENCE
Surmounted most expectations.
Great! Very moving.

HILL-TOP EXPERIENCE
A little less than a Mountain-top.
Fulfilled most expectations.

FLATLANDS
Average, run-of-the-mill experience.
No real highs or lows.

SWAMP
The pits. Far below expectations.
I need to climb out of this.

9:15 Cabin cleanup (for junior high only)
10:00 Morning meeting
11:15 Elective seminars
12:30 Lunch
1:30 Free time
4:30 Optional seminars
6:00 Dinner
7:00 Evening meeting
8:30 Evening activity (some groups reverse the order and have the evening activity first with the meeting afterward)
11:00 Lights out

Junior high usually requires more structure; therefore, we recommend the following adaptation of the preceding morning schedule:

7:00 Wake up
8:00 Breakfast
9:00 Cabin cleanup
9:40 Morning meeting
10:30 Organized individual activity (archery, riflery)
11:30 Special team competition
12:30 Lunch

CAMP TIME

Most teens complain about having to go to bed so early and get up so early. By establishing camp time, you can let them go to bed at 2 a.m. and get up at 9 a.m. Make the first matter of camp business the establishment of camp time. Have all the campers move their watches ahead two hours (maybe more or less). All activities will be held

according to camp time. Even though the teens know about the time change, they really respond to the new hours. This works most effectively at a week-long resident camp. *Ron Wells*

THE FIRST DAY

The most important day in camp is the first. Make sure the first impression is best by providing plenty of good food, varied and exciting activities, and quality content. Give the campers enough free time to explore and get acquainted with the surroundings. If travel has been long, have very short meetings and plenty of activity. The first message should be light, allowing the campers an insight into the speaker as a person as well as a preview of what's going to be discussed.

MEETINGS

• **Morning Meeting.** The morning meeting should be designed for maximum participation from the campers. The following suggestions represent some of the most effective ways to accomplish this:

—Precede the morning meeting with a personal or cabin devotional time where the passage for the morning can be studied and discussed. Then during the morning meeting the campers can share what they learned.

—Have the entire group watch a short role-play that presents an unresolved dilemma. Then have the campers meet in cabin groups or discussion groups and discuss the role-play. Bring the group back together again and have them share their conclusions. They could do the role-play again, changing it however they wanted.

• **Seminars.** Seminars are 1- to 1½-hour sessions on specialized subjects. There can be open seminars (no limit to the number that can attend) or closed seminars (limited attendance). A variety of seminars should be offered so that the campers have a good choice of topics. Seminars can be theology oriented (the Holy Spirit, the justice of God), issue oriented (materialism, sex), Bible oriented (study of Romans), or small-group oriented.

Limited seminars should offer class cards on a first-come-first-serve basis. When a class is full, campers can then attend their second choice. Total class cards should equal total number of campers.

• **Evening Meeting.** This meeting is the most important of the day. It should be looked forward to. A good evening meeting includes lots of singing, good fun, quality special music, and a lot of variety. It should not last longer than an hour and a half.

• **Lunchtime Fun.** Lunchtime can and should be the focal point of fun and information. It can include announcements of the afternoon schedule, special events, point totals, cabin cleanup, birthdays, skits, stunts, entertainment, and mail call. The following is typical of the lunchtime humor:

Cabin-Cleanup Fashion Show. All the items are modeled by the cabin inspector. The clothes have been found lying around the cabins. Sometimes the clothing must be helped out of a suitcase. As the week progresses campers begin to catch on and leave some of their friends' items out.

The cabin inspector puts on all the clothes at the same time. There should be a good combination of bathing suits, pajamas, robes, and nighties. By careful planning, the clothes can be put on in such a way that as each piece is taken off and given to the owner (who must claim it), the next item is seen for the first time. For example, you would have a bathing suit covered by a nightie covered by long john pajamas covered by a robe.

CAMP RECREATION

• **Non-Skilled Competitive Activities.** The most effective recreation program consists of a mixture of skilled and non-skilled competitive activities. Skilled competition, such as volleyball, baseball, and football, should be available on a voluntary basis during free time. Team competition or required recreation should be non-skilled, such as broom hockey, balloon basketball, American Eagle, etc. Non-skilled activities like those are fun to watch, fun to participate in, and never depend on ability.

Consider water carnivals, swim meets, water balloon events, boating events, snow activities, special events, and much more appropriate for camps and recreation.

• **Teams.** In camping situations longer than a weekend, it is desirable to divide the group into teams. Teams can benefit the camping program or be detrimental, depending on your view of competition. If every activity in camp is based on team competition, campers become polarized with the success or failure of camp resting on whether or not their team wins the competition. You can overcome this by:

—Limiting competitive activities to one or two a day.

—Allowing the first place team to compete first in all events. Almost always the teams following learn from the others' mistakes.

—Announcing competition results only once a day.

Names of teams can be anything from serious to ridiculous. Teams can elect captains, cheerleaders, mascots, and write their own cheers, fight songs, etc. The ridiculous teams can be anything from cartoons ("Peanuts") to their own creation (The Olive Pits). For serious names one group named their teams Faith, Love, Hope, and Charity. Each team was given a camcorder and told to make a short three-minute video (serious or humorous) that communicated the name of their team.

• **Points.** Points are free, so why give a team three points when you can give them 300 or 3000? When a team receives 3000 points, they really feel like they've won something.

Points can be given for just about anything. Remember, the important thing is not winning but having a good time. So don't overdo it. If one team is running away with the score, you can always even things out by giving penalty points, bonus points, etc.

Points can be used to recognize a variety of interests or skills:

—Polar Bear Swim: A delightful morning swim around 6 a.m. Those who manage to make it to the water then must fulfill certain requirements (swim out to the diving platform, etc.). These brave souls not only receive points for their team, but they also receive a membership card in the Polar Bear Club.

—Midnight Swim: Another chilly way to spend the late evening.

—Mountain Climb: A semi-difficult march through some rugged terrain for points and membership card.

The weekly team winner can receive a special prize, such as an ice cream sundae, but most of the time winning is enough.

RULES

Rules are a necessary part of every camp. Many church camps suffer from an overabundance of rules, however. Too many rules and you begin to create more problems than you prevent. Certainly we cannot dictate a specific set of rules, but we can give you some important guidelines for establishing your own set.

• The fewer the better. Many rules do not need to be mentioned. The kids already know they cannot bring drugs to camp, for example.

• Do not try to establish your authority by a stern demeanor or an authoritarian lecture. Make the rules light, firm with a slight touch of humor. (Instead of saying, "No rocks thrown in the lake," say "We have a game that you are not allowed to play at camp; it's called 'bomb the duck.'")

• Never bluff. When you announce certain consequences for breaking a rule, be sure to carry it out. It is better to keep quiet about punishment and deal with each situation individually.

• Deal with situations as they arise privately with those involved. Public flogging happened in the Middle Ages. Stay away from punishments that involve the entire camp. Public incidents that cause the whole camp to suffer can ruin the entire experience for the campers.

• Never deprive a camper of food, sleep, or shelter. Rules should be stated positively to create the understanding that they are for the betterment of the camping experience. Rules are not set to force people to act like Christians.

CAMP LEADERSHIP

• **The Dean.** The dean's responsibilities are to coordinate the total recreation and entertainment function of the program. This person is the platform personality and makes all decisions regarding the program. The dean is the liaison between the campground personnel and the program personnel, and is in charge of all counselor meetings.

• **Boy's Dean and Girl's Dean.** These two handle most of the discipline (except in serious cases which require involvement by the dean). Their main responsibility is to check cabins after lights out and make periodic checks during meetings.

• **Speaker.** The speaker presents much of the content of the conference. One meeting per day should be the maximum expected of this person for the general meetings. Seminars or electives allow

the campers freedom not to hear the speaker again. Of course, speakers can teach seminars or electives to a smaller group, but too much exposure can hurt their effectiveness. You should always provide the speaker with the following:

—Private lodging and restroom
—Bedding and linens
—Free time
—Honorarium (previously agreed upon) before he or she leaves

• **Recreation Director.** This person is in charge of all recreation regardless of whether it is competitive or free time. The director also organizes team competition that involves judging, point totals, rules, and equipment.

• **Counselors.** The counselors' responsibilities should not be limited to the actual time spent at camp. Ideally, there should be a relationship begun before camp and continued long after camp is over. *Relationship, leadership,* and *responsibility* are the key words for the effective counselor. First of all, the counselor is there to build a close relationship with the camper that, hopefully, will result in an atmosphere of openness and trust. It is the counselor's responsibility, secondly, to discern where leadership is needed to guide the camper toward growth. Of course, it is after camp when the counselor can be of real help by encouraging and making time available to be together. Counselors should be at least college age, be from the same church, and be well trained.

COOK-GROUP CHECKLISTS

Here's a great retreat idea if your kids are going to be cooking their own food. Divide the campers into small cook groups, which could be cabin groups, or family groups, or whatever. Each group is then assigned a meal that they must prepare and serve to the rest of the camp.

To make the actual cooking, serving, and cleanup go smoothly for each group, prepare in advance some checklists with detailed step-by-step instructions for preparing and serving each meal. It really takes the guesswork out of it for the kids, gives everyone something to do, and eliminates mistakes that can often ruin a meal. The students will really appreciate it, and so will you. Follow the samples to make up your own for the particular menu that you will be using.

Friday Dinner

_____ Put away refrigerator foods.

_____ Put out tablecloth.

_____ Heat up soup (3 cans vegetable).

_____ Mix up ½ gallon fruit punch.

_____ Set out napkins, spoons, and bowls.

_____ Pour 7 glasses of punch.

_____ Serve soup.

_____ Clean up: spoons, glasses, cooking pot, table, floors.

_____ Mix up another ½ gallon punch for Sat. lunch.

Friday Snack

_____ Heat up popcorn popper with cooking oil to line indicated.

_____ Heat up ½ stick butter if desired.

_____ Heat up water for hot chocolate or tea.

_____ Use only ½ cup popcorn per batch. Pour it in, and watch very carefully. Pour into grocery bag as soon as it stops popping (before it burns).

_____ Pour butter and salt over popcorn sparingly.

_____ Use one packet of hot chocolate mix per cup. Add water and stir very well.

_____ Serve snacks, along with napkins.

_____ Clean up: cups, popcorn popper, etc.

Saturday Breakfast

_____ Mix up pancake mix according to directions.

_____ Set out on table: stick of margarine, syrup (one bottle), knives, forks, napkins.

_____ Use 14 sausage links (2 per person). Cook in oven at 400 degrees for 30 minutes. Drain on paper towels.

_____ Use ½ gallon milk. Pour into 7 glasses and set on table.

_____ Mix up one can orange juice; pour into 7 small cups and put on table.

_____ It would be best to keep the plates in the kitchen and serve the pancakes on them. In other words, take a plate with 3 pancakes to each person.

_____ Your family is in charge of morning prayers. Be creative.

_____ Clean up: dishes, cups, griddle, table, floors, etc.

Saturday Lunch

_____ Heat up chili (3 or 4 cans).

_____ Put on a big pot of water to heat up a pack of hot dogs.

_____ Set out on table: hot dog buns, mustard, ketchup, as well as 7 plates, knives, forks, and napkins.

_____ Chop finely one onion.

_____ Set out potato chips in serving bowl.

_____ Pour out 7 cups of already chilled punch; set out on table.

_____ Your group is in charge of table grace.

_____ Mix up another ½ gallon fruit punch for dinner.

_____ Clean up: plates, utensils, cooking pots, table, floors.

_____ Dessert: Set out 21 cookies (3 per person).

Saturday Dinner

_____ Cook hamburger for taco filling according to package directions. Add a can of tomato sauce. Drain grease before adding.

_____ Shred lettuce.

_____ Grate cheddar cheese.

_____ Get out rest of chopped onion from lunch.

_____ Chop tomatoes. (3 of them to start)

_____ Set out on table: 7 plates, forks, and napkins, as well as taco sauce.

_____ Pour and set on table: 7 glasses of fruit punch.

_____ Warm up shells according to directions.

_____ Set out all food, including the chips.

_____ Your family is in charge of all table prayers.

_____ Clean up: cooking utensils, plates, forks, table, floor, etc.

_____ Mix up another ½ gallon of punch for tomorrow.

Sunday Breakfast

_____ Mix up 7 eggs and ¼ cup of milk to make french toast.

_____ Use rest of sausage links (2 per person). Cook in oven at 400 degrees for 30 minutes. Drain on paper towels.

_____ Dip bread (14 pieces to start) in egg mixture and fry on griddle.

_____ Set out on table: 7 plates, forks, glasses, and napkins. Also set out: syrup, margarine.

_____ Set out 7 glasses of milk.

_____ Mix up orange juice and pour into small glasses.

_____ Your family is in charge of morning table grace.

_____ Clean up everything: plates, cooking utensils, table, floors.

Rhonda C. Knight

HOT CHOCOLATE FOR 50

Here's a much less expensive alternative to the pre-mixed hot chocolate that kids love on retreats. The recipe serves 50. Mix in desired quantities, but in this proportion:

> 8 qt water
> Dry milk (correct amount for 8 qt water)
> 1 lb Nestles Quik
> 1 lb confectioners' sugar
> 6 oz dry (non-dairy) creamer
> ½ tsp salt
> ½ tsp nutmeg

David Washburn

CANNED COOKOUT

Here's a unique way to cook hamburgers, bacon and eggs, or whatever you like to cook outdoors. Items needed are an empty three-pound coffee can, some dry sticks, paper for burning, matches, and, of course, the food.

Take the empty coffee can with one end opened. Cut a hole on the side of the can three inches in diameter. Cut up from the opened end. On the opposite side of the can near the top, punch holes for the smoke to go out when burning. Gather sticks and paper and fill the can loosely; turn upside down (opened end on ground) and

start a fire to the paper and sticks. When the flame is going, begin frying on the top of the can. It works! _Betty Horgen_

INTEREST-EARNING SIGN-UPS

With a little advance planning you can cut student costs for retreats, while at the same time making it easier for you to spend more money on improving events.

About six to 12 months before a retreat, request registration payments from your students. At that time offer registrants a monthly payment plan that concludes the month prior to the retreat. It's easier for the kids to come up with small amounts at intervals—plus it builds anticipation for the retreat.

As soon as you receive advance registration, invest the money to receive interest to be used to cover the cost of the retreat (or other events). For example, if you charge $100 per student for a retreat and you expect 15 youths to attend, you could expect the following return:
- $20 down multiplied by 15 students equals $300.
- $10 per student in monthly payments for eight months equals $1200.
- Deposited in a savings account that calculates monthly at 5 percent, the investment would produce an extra $28.
- The return increases with more money down, longer-term savings, more frequent payments, a higher interest rate, and a larger group.

Do one better—show your students the numbers and let them designate the interest money to world relief or missions. *Len Cuthbert*

CLEANUP DEPOSIT

If your church owns or rents a vehicle for youth trips, you know how fast trash can accumulate in it. Usually the youth leader gets stuck cleaning it up.

Why not consider a cleanup deposit for your next trip? Before the trip ask for five dollars (or whatever amount you choose) as a deposit to insure a clean bus or van. *Everyone* forfeits their deposit if the vehicle is trashy, even if it's not their trash. *Greg Miller*

LOVE LETTERS

After an overnighter or retreat, write parents letters telling them how their teens behaved on the trip. This is especially good for kids who never cause trouble. This compliments campers for good behavior and gives parents feedback on their child's behavior. *James C. Harville, Jr.*

TYPES OF CAMPS AND RETREATS

TABERNACLIN' RETREAT

The Old Testament tabernacle was more than a place of worship—it symbolized quiet, reflection, and study.

So plan a retreat along these lines: invite a guest speaker who will not only instruct your group about personal worship, but lead them in developing the habit. Perhaps your speaker could teach your kids through a short book on the subject. Of course, give your teenagers plenty of quiet solitude during this kind of a retreat in order to practice what the guest speaker has taught.

And be sure that your retreat schedule includes times for "Group Tabernaclin'" and "Manna"! *Greg Fiebig*

CHURCH LOCK-IN

The Church Lock-In is an experiment in Christian education that is designed to give kids an intensive one-week experience of personal growth, fellowship, and study. Normally this is done away from the church, like at a camp or retreat, but at a Church Lock-In, the kids live at the church for an entire week. It should begin on a Monday and run through Saturday during the summer, Easter vacation, or whenever kids are out of school for a week. Sleeping rooms should be set up with cots, rollaways, air mattresses, sleeping bags, or however the kids choose to sleep. All meals are either prepared at the church or catered (Kentucky Fried Chicken, etc.). Perhaps the final meal (banquet) can be a giant potluck, with the families joining the kids for an evening program.

The daily routine of the lock-in can be patterned after the following daily schedule used by one youth group:

8:00-8:30 a.m. Breakfast is served. Make it simple, like cold cereal, orange juice, breakfast rolls. Maybe fix scrambled eggs one morning (with sausage, etc.). Breakfast may be preceded with a few exercises to loosen everybody up.

8:30-10:00 a.m. Study at the church. Get the kids a good textbook (paperback) that you can cover in a week's time. Pick a good theme such as the Life of Christ, Christian Values, the Seven Last Words of Christ (for Easter week), which can be a day-to-day study. The kids should use this time to read and study the text, take notes, use their Bibles, write down questions they might have, and so on. It should be a time of personal study.

10:00-12:00 a.m. This can be a follow-up time to the personal study period that preceded. It can vary in method every day. One day can be a trip to the public library where the kids can find other references to deepen their understanding of the subject. They can be instructed to use the card catalog and the Reader's Guide to locate relevant books and periodicals. The kids can then share with each other what they found. Another day can feature a film on the subject under study, or a special speaker. If there is a Bible college or seminary nearby, perhaps the kids can visit classes or have the professors come and share insights. Other days can include discussion groups, role-playing, and other ways of digging into the meanings of the subject at hand.

12:00-12:30 p.m. Lunch.

12:30-7:00 p.m. During the afternoon, a variety of activities can be planned for each day. During the summer, when the weather is hot, swimming at a public or privately owned swimming pool can be part of every afternoon's schedule. Other activities can include the following:

—Service projects: Ministering to the needy, doing work projects for poor or disabled or needy people in the community; working around the church (janitorial or repairing, painting, etc.); visiting convalescent homes.

—Special events: Treasure hunts, kite-flying contests, bike trips, etc.

—Field trips: Amusement parks, the zoo, the beach, the mountains, the art museum, other interesting or fun places within driving distance.

—Playing games: Indoor games (Scrabble, Monopoly, Ping-Pong, etc.) Give each kid 20 tickets at the beginning of the games, and at the end of the games (or the week) whoever has the most tickets wins a prize. Every time you lose a game, you have to give one of your tickets to the winner of the game.

—Cleaning up: One day (at least) the kids should be allowed to go home or somewhere to shower and wash up, perhaps take naps.

7:00-7:30 p.m. Dinner.

7:30-on. Singing, films, skits, fun, fellowship, etc., followed up with rap sessions, discussions, special guests (music groups, speakers, etc.), question-and-answer periods, and the like.

A Church Lock-In can be a refreshing change of pace from the traditional camp or retreat, and in some cases, the kids grow to appreciate their church building a little more, after spending a week living in it. Also, this is a great way to get maximum usage out of your church's facilities.

Remember to have plenty of counselors—a good ratio is one to eight—and to train them well, just as you would for a normal camp. Be creative in every area of your planning, and expect a great week. *Gary Smith*

A.C.T.S. RETREAT

This is an idea for a retreat that deals primarily with the topic of prayer. The letters A.C.T.S. stand for *Adoration, Confession, Thanksgiving,* and *Supplication,* four basic ingredients of prayer. Each day should consist of some intense Bible study on prayer and, of course, lots of time for prayer itself. Each day could focus on the four ingredients. It can be a very effective retreat. *Ron Elliot*

SPECIAL DAYS CAMP

To give a junior high camp some distinctiveness, designate each day as a special day. Activities and dress can be geared to that special day. Here are some suggestions for special days with appropriate ideas:

• **Nature Day.** Hike, nature scavenger hunt, picnic, night walk.

• **Backwards Day.** Reverse schedule for the day, reverse the meals, wear clothes backwards, walk backwards to all activities.

• **Western Day.** Stage a holdup with counselors dressed up as bandits, follow with counselor hunt by campers, then gold hunt (rocks sprayed with gold paint).

• **Skit Day.** Have skits by counselors, by campers, by other staff.

• **Christmas in June (July, or August).** Celebrate by exchanging names, making crafts to give as presents, Christmas drama, Christmas carols.

• **Native American Day.** Dress up with homemade headbands and bead bracelets or anklets, horseback riding, Thanksgiving drama, archery, tracking through the woods, nature or clay crafts. *William Moore*

CAMPING WITH EXPERTS

If your camp is relatively small, you may benefit from the free services of experts in the field of nature. A forest ranger will gladly take your campers on a nature hike, explain to them how to determine the age of a tree, and identify local trees. The Department of Natural Resources will send out people from their section on Fisheries and Game to talk about the different fish in the lake or animals that inhabit the forest. If there is a scuba-diving outfit in town, they will usually send out someone to give a free scuba-diving demonstration. *William C. Moore*

SPECIALIZED CAMPS

• **Travel Camps.** Travel camps or caravan camps are simply conferences where the entire group moves to a new location every day. The campers travel in buses, campers, station wagons, cars, or bikes. Depending on the time allowed, each day's schedule consists of some travel time, sightseeing, and a meeting. Some days may just be sightseeing and activities. The important thing about travel camps is the flexibility of the schedule. You play it by ear each day. Let the location determine what your activities will be. If the group is tired, then you sleep in.

• **Water-Ski Trip.** Water-ski trips can be very effective for outreach or for introducing new kids to your church youth group. One approach is to make the trip a one-on-one experience. Each church

young person should bring one unchuched young person in order to attend. He must also attend two orientation meetings that cover the basic steps for sharing one's faith in Christ.

—**Schedule:** It's simple— water-ski, breakfast, water-ski, lunch, water-ski, dinner, water-ski, meeting, sleep.

—**Boats:** You need one boat per 10 campers. Recruit boats from church members, outside people, or anyone who has a boat and is willing to attend. You should pay all their expenses.

—**Food:** Don't skimp on food. The best arrangement is to set up cook groups of about 10 to 12 kids. Each group elects a cook captain. They are responsible to see that their group has enough cooking utensils, barbecue grill, etc., for the group. Each camper brings her own eating utensils and washes her own dishes. There is a control kitchen tent. The food is given out at certain times, and it is given to the captains only.

—**Cost:** Even with good quality food, you can usually keep the costs quite low. The important thing is that your costs cover the expenses, because a water-ski trip will not be difficult with kids anxious to pay the price.

• **Snow-Ski Trip.** This is another one-on-one conference with the same requirements for attendance as the water-ski trip. A good time to schedule this would be Monday through Wednesday during Christmas vacation. Try to book a chalet dormitory. It is much cheaper than any ski club. The equipment can be rented, and you can instruct dryland lessons. Of course, in many areas of the country everyone knows how to ski. And for some help with community building during the ski trip, use the Ski-Trip Affirmation and Holy Lift Ticket ideas in the Programming chapter of this book.

• **Overnight Camp-Out.** This is a simple camp. Camp at a campground near a beach or lake on Friday night. For dinner have hamburgers, sodas, etc. Keep it simple. The rest of the evening include a campfire, ghost story, games, songs, and a devotion led by one of the kids or the youth director. Saturday morning have breakfast rolls or donuts, juice, and milk. Spend the day at the beach or lake and have hot dogs for lunch. Go home Saturday night.

LOGOS CAMP

This is a different approach to summer camp. This "Summer Seminar in Christian Living" called Logos is designed to strengthen the body of Christ rather than emphasizing evangelism as most summer camps do. An excerpt from the brochure for the camp originally using this idea: "The purpose of the Summer Seminar is to equip members of the college-career fellowship with the necessary guidelines to shine as true beacon lights for God in a dark and dying world through a more vital and committed daily relationship with him and with fellow members of the body of Christ." The camping day includes three main sessions:

• Upreach—the Christian's relationship to God
• Outreach—the Christian's relationship to the non-believer
• Inreach—the Christian's relationship to the body of Christ

Bob Griffin

CONCENTRATION CAMP

Have a weekend study retreat with a maximum of teaching, Bible study, discussion, and planning and a minimum of fun and games. Call it a Concentration Camp and invite any kid who really wants to dig in for a couple days. This is particularly good at the beginning of the school year. *Richard McPherson*

PARENT–TEEN CAMP

The following retreat idea has been used with great success in establishing a family ministry in the youth program. In order to attend, there must be at least one teenager and one parent from the same family. The camp begins on Friday at 9:00 p.m. and ends on Saturday at 8:30 p.m. This short schedule allows parents to get away and keeps costs down.

Friday:	9:00 p.m.	All together, guest speaker, crowd breakers, and fun film
	10:00-10:30 p.m.	Snack time
Saturday:	8:00 a.m.	Breakfast
	9:00 a.m.	Parents—guest speaker, kids—youth leader

10:00 a.m.	Break
10:30 a.m.	Meet together, guest speaker
11:30 a.m.	Recreation
12:15 p.m.	Lunch
1:30 p.m.	Film or activity
2:00 p.m.	Discussions in group
3:00 p.m.	Free time
5:00 p.m.	Dinner
6:00 p.m.	Leave for home

The first night, some crowd breakers and a fun film will help loosen everyone up, especially the parents. You can bring along a guest speaker who is good with families to share a short message and spend the rest of the evening just in fellowship. Have fathers room with sons, mothers with daughters, etc. You can work this any way you want.

The next day, two meetings are scheduled. The first can be with parents and kids, separated and talked to as individual groups, then everyone meets together in one group for a rap session with the guest speaker. Recreation can include volleyball (parents must hold hands with their kids—really wild). Basketball can also be a good family game: fathers and gals versus mothers and guys.

During the afternoon, show a film or do an activity that promotes discussion about family communication. After this, families meet and discuss pressures in their families. It usually takes a while for these to get going, but the results are great. After 45 minutes, the families join together in the large group to share what they feel has been accomplished. Then, discuss ways that the families can do things to understand each other better. Kids can share what they like to do with their parents or what they like about their parents and vice-versa. For a short but effective retreat, the long-range results of this type of thing can be very good. *Jim Grindle*

BLIND RETREAT

There are many experiences that help sensitize young people to the problems of others. This idea is outstanding for that purpose, but requires careful planning and preparation of the participants. Kids at a retreat are blindfolded securely with gauze and bandages for an 18-hour period. During that time only the sponsors of the group can see, and must help the kids function without their sight. They must eat, sleep, dress, play, and communicate without the use of their eyes for the entire length of time.

The results are astounding. For some kids, the experience is extremely frightening, and they should be allowed to remove the blindfolds if they just can't handle it any longer. But for the kids who stick it out, they are able to understand more fully the plight of the blind and the beauty of sight. Kids do improve at getting along without their eyes as time goes along, but they really learn what it means to be dependent on others.

Follow up the experience with discussion and a study of Scripture passages relating to blindness and a worship service thanking God for sight and the beauty of his creation.

Be sure that safety precautions are taken to prevent accidents that might occur from kids bumping into things, stumbling, or falling.

WAGON TRAIN

Here's a new twist to an old idea, great as a different kind of camping experience. Secure the use of an open field and enlist several truck or trailer campers or motorhomes. Park them in a circle. Have a campfire within the circle, with plenty of food, hot chocolate, games, singing, and spiritual thought. It's a great overnight retreat. *Danny Dye*

REVOLVING DOOR CAMP

Many times when you plan a camp, you discover that some people can't come for the entire week because of jobs or finances, but they would like to come for a day or two, or some other part of it. Usually that only creates problems, since you like to have some continuity with most camp programs, and it's hard when people come and go.

But what if you just planned a camp with that in mind? This would be especially appropriate with older youths—like college students—who are usually broke, have summer jobs, etc. Plan a camp in which students can come whenever they can. Hold it somewhere that is close, charge them by the meal, by the day (or night), and plan programs and activities that can be done by any number, and

aren't presented in a series of some kind.

One group did this by reserving a group camping area at a local beach during the summer. A main supply tent was set up with food and a place for kids to change clothes, and those who came just brought a sleeping bag and slept out. Everybody cooked their own food on open fires or camp stoves, and the overall response was better than any other camp the group had ever done. One or two adult couples remained there the entire week, but they were the only live-in campers. Everyone else came when they could. Use your own creativity and this type of camp can be a real success for your group, too. *Wilber Griffith*

BASIC TRAINING

Try a military theme for your next retreat by calling it Boot Camp and using military jargon throughout the weekend. Begin the event with In-Processing, where the kids are registered and given matching T-shirts which they must wear at all times. (You can create a special logo for the shirts with your group's name and the words BASIC TRAINING.) When kids are *dismissed*, they must report to the

barracks (cabin or meeting room) to learn the basic training motto: "Highly motivated, truly dedicated, rough, tough, can't get enough, praise God!" The first meal served that evening is *C-rations*.

Divide the *trainees* into *squads*, each with a *squad leader* from the staff and an enthusiastic *assistant squad leader* from the group. Have each squad choose a name, mascot, color, motto, and Bible verse. Squad times can be used for devotions, discussion, reviews, or skit preparation. Design training exercises such as *Bible marksmanship* (locating verses), and have the squads compete. Call large group meetings for teaching and worship *mission briefings*.

If you can locate a trumpet and player, rouse the troops in the morning with a genuine *reveille*, and start the day with *PT*—stretching and light exercise followed by a short jog. Create your own *cadence* for the group to chant as they run.

End the weekend with a *USO Show* of skits planned and performed by squads, individual youth, and staff. Be sure to take lots of pictures throughout the weekend so you can follow up later with a slide show of kids' first boot camp. *Joan Nusbaum*

PUBLICITY

CAMP WALL

Put peer pressure to work for you! Promote camp registration by creating a camp wall—an entire wall in your meeting room that you creatively decorate. For example, first cover the wall with colorful paper or fabric, and then paint or paste on it your camp logo, photos from the previous year, etc. Call the wall by the name of your camp—Bear Mountain Wall, Victory Wall, etc.

Most of your camp wall, however, will be devoted to all the names of your teens. As they register, somehow highlight their names on the wall. The students really will look forward to seeing their name lit up—especially if surrounding names are already highlighted. *Ron Sylvia*

UP BOARD

Camps and retreats are usually up experiences for a youth group. So why not benefit from them all year round? Have the group create an Up Board—a bulletin board reserved for photos and other mementos from past camps, retreats, or other mountaintop highs that the group has had. Whenever someone is feeling a little down they should get a real lift from looking at the Up Board. *Donna McElrath*

CAMP KIDNAP LETTER

Here's a clever letter idea that can be used both for promotion and as a camp registration and parental permission form. Letters and words are cut from a magazine, pasted down, and printed up in the following manner:

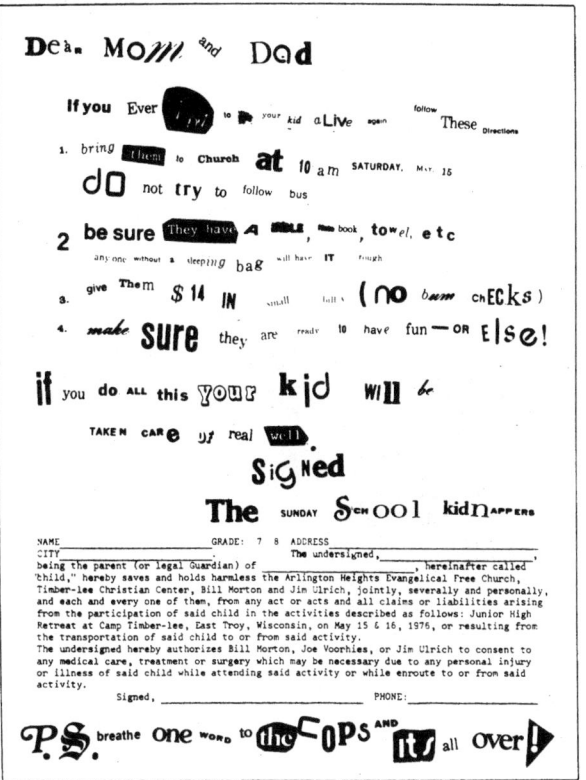

Jim Ulrich

WHAT REALLY HAPPENED?

Help kids in your youth group who didn't attend the last retreat to feel included by playing What Really Happened? at the next meeting. Set this game up like a TV game show—contestants are those who weren't at the retreat. Sit them behind a table and give them all two cards, one that says "True" and the other "False."

Then those who did attend the retreat take turns posing statements of what happened—and what supposedly happened. Contestants must hold up the card that reflects their opinion of each statement. You may want to keep track of points and award prizes—including one for a group member whose statement stumps the entire panel of contestants. *Cinda Gorman*

SLEEPING-BAG ANNOUNCEMENT

Here's a creative way to announce a slumber party, church lock-in, overnight retreat, or camp. Send your invitations in a sleeping bag.

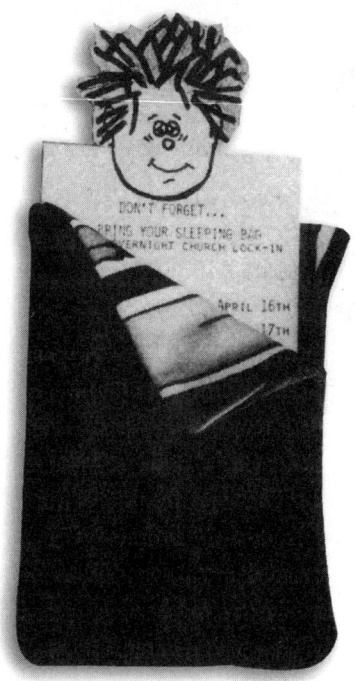

Have an adult or youth who can sew make individual bags for each announcement. Two scraps of fabric—one of them a print and both of them about nine inches by seven inches—should be sewn together to make a mini-bag.

Sewing instructions:

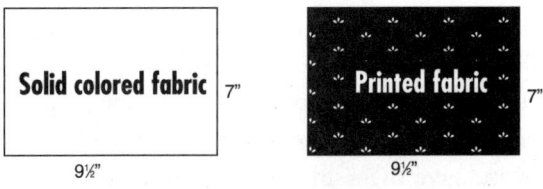

With right sides together, sew the solid colored fabric to the printed fabric. Sew around three sides.

The announcements can be drawn with a sleepy face on top and slipped into the bag. Pass these out or lay them out on a table for the kids to pick up and give to friends. *Annette W. Glosson*

MOUNTAINTOP INSURANCE

Young people are often disappointed when they come home from camp because their families or parents are not prepared for them. Kids who have been away for a week of camp usually have mountaintop experiences that are very meaningful and important for them—but when they return home, no one seems to notice. This often leaves them frustrated and wondering whether or not anything significant really happened at all.

The situation can be avoided by sending a letter to the parents of each young person before camp begins to alert them of the problem. Such a letter can help parents be more sensitive to the emotional needs of their children when they return home from camp. Here is a suggested format:

> Dear Parents,
> We in the youth department of (church) believe that youth ministry involves not only the students themselves, but their families as well. So we would like to take this opportunity to share with you a little bit about the camp your child is attending this week. We are hoping this week will be one of real growth, and that your child will experience God's love in a new and exciting way.
>
> What will we be doing at camp? Well, there will be many activities, but the most important of all will be our evening campfires. We have invited a guest speaker, (name), who will be sharing with the kids each night. At these meetings, and in cabin groups throughout the week, we will be encouraging our young people to think seriously about their relationships to Christ and to make or renew a commitment to him.
>
> There is a good chance that your child will have what we sometimes call a mountaintop experience while away at camp. So it's important that our youths return to an environment that is warm and supportive. Although your life may not have changed at all during the week, your child will have probably been questioning, searching, and making some big decisions. Your teenager will be emotionally high and may want to share some thoughts and feelings with you. Your child will be different, even if only for a few days or weeks. When the emotions of being close to friends and God wear off, you can encourage your child to apply what has been learned and offer your support just by listening.
>
> We love our youths very much, and hope to have a continuing, positive relationship with both them and you.
>
> Sincerely in Christ,
> Gail Harris

Of course, you will want to tailor your letter to your own situation, and to the details of your camp or retreat. Letters can be written individually, or you can just print up a form letter for larger groups. Such an approach will help make that transition from the mountaintop to the real world a little easier for your kids. *Gail Harris*

CAMP CHARIOTS

This is a good idea if you are having a camp that involves a number of youth groups or if you are having team competition and want to generate a little excitement prior to camp. Send a notice to the participating groups asking each to construct a chariot that can be brought to camp for the colossal chariot race that will be held during camp. The chariot can be constructed out of anything and should be designed so that four people do the pulling and one person rides. Not only will the chariots be raced, but awards will be given for most imaginative, best design, ugliest, etc. Any size group can bring a chariot to race, and if the group is large, one chariot can be entered for every 10 people in the group. This event not only provides a fun activity at camp, but really helps in the promotion of it as well. *John Tolle*

ON THE ROAD

FOOT FACES

On your next long drive to or from camp, take along some colorful markers (with tips of varying sizes) and have teens with artistic talent create wild drawings on the feet of volunteers. Be sure to take pictures of the finished masterpieces for the next slide show. *Richard Moore*

SHOPPING SPREE

Here is an idea that saves you lots of time and is a fun way to begin a weekend retreat. Instead of buying all of the food for the retreat in advance and transporting it in bulky bags and leaking ice chests to the retreat site, buy the food at a supermarket near the retreat site after you arrive. The entire youth group can get into the act if you all go together. Give everyone a shopping list with two or three items to bring to designated shopping carts located near the checkout stand. Award a prize to the fastest shopper and the one who brings back the best bargain! *Stephen Williams*

TRIP PACKETS

A good way to pass the time on long trips is to give each traveler a creative trip packet filled with items such as these:

• **Trip guidebook.** Create a book that contains a list of trip counselors, a trip schedule, new choruses, a letter from the youth pastor, announcements for future youth group events, a principle page (rules for the trip), and pages for taking notes, devotional notes, and getting autographs and addresses.

• **Brochure of retreat center or motel.**

• **Christian music cassette/CD.** Get music on sale at your local Christian bookstore or at a discount from record companies when one of their artists is coming to your area.

• **Puzzles and games.** Include ones that require teamwork. Offer prizes to winners.

• **Fliers of upcoming events.** Jesus-festival fliers, rallies in the area, high school outreaches, Christian skate nights, etc.

• **Interesting tracts.** Generate discussion on the trip with creative tracts from your local Christian bookstore.

• **Candy.** What more can we say about candy?

Place these items in large envelopes or decorated paper bags. Create additional enclosures that are unique to your group.

Robert Crosby

ENCOURAGEMENT BEANS

During a long bus trip or on a retreat, you can have some fun as well as teach your group how to encourage each other and praise another's good deeds. First give each student 20 beans. Explain that more beans can be earned in the following ways:

• By giving a sincere and encouraging word to another person. (Flattery—that is, giving words of praise for personal gain—is not rewarded.)

• By kind or helpful actions.

• By good attitudes while working or participating.

Beans are awarded by leaders under the following conditions:

• When they observe kids encouraging others by their actions, words, or attitudes.

• When a young person observes an encouraging

action, word, or attitude and tells a leader. In this case not only the encourager but perhaps even the reporter will earn a bean.

Beans can be confiscated by leaders when they observe discouraging actions, words, or attitudes (for example, criticizing, complaining, ridiculing, showing disrespect).

Students who receive a discouraging action, word, or attitude may request a bean from the offender, provided they do not reciprocate with an unkind action, word, or attitude, and simply smile politely and hold out their hands.

Here's what a student may do who observes discouraging actions, words, or attitudes:
1. If an observer tattles to a leader, the tattletale loses a bean to the leader.
2. Before reporting the offender to a leader, the observing student must ask the offender to turn himself in to the leader or confess the discouraging action, word, or attitude to the observer himself.
3. If the offender refuses at the first opportunity to admit his wrong to a leader or another student, then the observer may report him to a leader without incurring the tattletale penalty.
4. If an offender admits his wrong, he loses one bean; if he refuses to admit and is consequently reported, he loses two beans.

To remind the kids that being encouraging pays, announce that the ones with the most beans at the end of the trip or retreat receive rewards. *Ed Laremore*

GUARDIAN ANGELS

This relationship-building idea is useful at camps or retreats. At the first session, assign same-sex partners. Partners should not know each other very well. Explain that each kid is his partner's guardian angel. Partners must sit together at specified sessions and eat certain meals together. They must also pray for each other and perform at least one act of Christian service for the other person during the retreat. At the end of the retreat, have some of the kids describe what happened. Chances are that kids will form some lasting friendships.

Or guardian angels can be secretly assigned. Acts of kindness are to be done anonymously. Identities can be revealed later. *Paul Tonna*

PAY TOILET

Tired of being only 15 minutes down the road to camp when you start getting pleas to stop for potty breaks? Before the bus leaves the church, negotiate

with your kids the amount that everyone leaving the bus for restroom use must pay. When you do stop (probably every few hours, now), kids pay as they exit the bus for a restroom—and you pocket a tidy sum for the church missions offering. *Greg Fiebig*

CRAZY COUPONS

On your next retreat, distribute official coupon books to all kids. The books are great for laughs

and for getting people to interact. The only rules are:
• You cannot refuse to redeem a coupon when asked.
• A different person must redeem each of your coupons.
• The other person must sign the coupon when redeemed, but you get to keep it as a souvenir.

Carolyn Roddy

FOR BETTER OR FOR VERSE

Here is a possible way to form small groups for a retreat. Beforehand, choose some Bible verses and, depending on the number of people per group, write a word or phrase from the verse on separate 3x5 cards. To identify the verse place the book on one card and the chapter and verse on another. Finally, randomly distribute the cards and let the kids form the verses. Each group is created by the kids who hold cards from the same verse. *Jim Shewmaker and Steve Kraftchick*

EXAMPLE: John 15:1

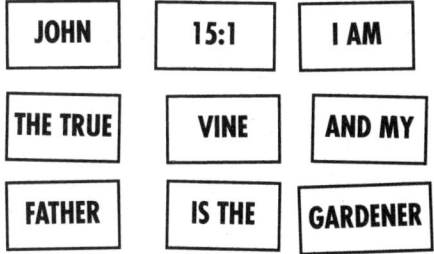

JOHN	15:1	I AM
THE TRUE	VINE	AND MY
FATHER	IS THE	GARDENER

IT'S HUG TIME

Tell campers about a new rule you have created. Whenever they hear your alarm clock sound off, they must yell "It's hug time!" and hug as many people as possible before the alarm stops. Carry your clock with you wherever you go and set it off when large or small groups of kids are nearby. *Jan Schaibl*

FRAGILE FRIENDS

This exercise can make kids aware of the fragility of other people and the importance of being gentle with each other. It is appropriate for use at a camp or retreat.

Give each person a raw egg. Have kids try to remove the contents of the eggs without cracking the shells by using a pin or nail to punch a small hole in each end of each egg. The contents of each egg will be forced out the other end, leaving empty, unbroken eggshells. You can seal the eggs with a small amount of candle wax. Save the insides of the eggs for use at breakfast the next morning. Discuss the delicate nature of eggshells and

relate this to the delicate nature of our relationships with each other. Then give kids fine-point markers to write on the eggshells. Have kids carefully write the names of several kids in the group on the eggshell (don't break the eggs).

Kids must carry their eggs with them all day or for a set amount of time. They must protect their eggs until you collect them. Discuss the egg activity and how it relates to protecting relationships. *Audrey Quinn*

IT'S INEDIBLE

Sing this song at summer camp to the old Perry Como hit "It's Impossible," to commemorate glorious camp food.

It's Inedible

It's inedible! Call it food if you desire, but it's inedible!
It's incredible how it sets my heart on fire—it's just incredible!
As I force it closer to me, I can feel it oozing through me;
With each mouthful I'm reminded that it's really quite inedible.

It's inedible! Just by looking you can tell that it's inedible.
It's incredible—oh, how dreadful it can smell; it's just incredible!
And tomorrow, when the aftertaste is gone, I'll still regret it,
For no matter how I try I can't forget it!

So believe me when I say it's just inedible.

It's inedible! Bring the stomach pumps with haste, 'cuz it's inedible!
It's incredible how offensive it can taste—it's just incredible!
And tomorrow, please forgive me if my state of health is dismal,
For it seems that I've run out of Pepto-Bismol;

And that proves beyond a doubt that it's inedible!
Steve Jones

31

Scripture Schedule

Use this camp exercise to get your kids into the Scriptures as soon as they get off of the bus. Give each camper a list of times that contains clues about the upcoming week's schedule. Kids must search the Bible for answers to the clues. Add or change verses or times as needed.

Sample Scripture Schedule

7:00 a.m.—Jonah 1:6 *(Rise and shine)*
7:45 a.m.—Psalm 5:3 *(Morning prayer and praise)*
8:00 a.m.—1 Timothy 6:8 *(Breakfast)*
8:30 a.m.—John 9:4 *(Chores)*
9:00 a.m.—Psalm 8:3a *(Craft project)*
10:00 a.m.—2 Timothy 2:15 *(Class)*
11:00 a.m.—2 Samuel 2:14 *(Recreation)*
12:00 p.m.—Ephesians 5:19 *(Chapel)*
12:45 p.m.—Matthew 4:4 *(Lunch)*
1:30 p.m.—2 Thessalonians 3:10 *(Chores)*
2:30 p.m.—Job 40:20 *(Recreation)*
4:30 p.m.—Luke 11:41b *(Camp cleanup)*
5:30 p.m.—Revelation 19:9 *(Dinner)*
6:30 p.m.—2 Chronicles 34:12a *(Chores)*
7:00 p.m.—Psalm 42:8 *(Vespers)*
7:45 p.m.—Psalm 100:1-2 *(Music)*
8:30 p.m.—Zechariah 8:5 *(Recreation)*
10:00 p.m.—Psalm 63:5-7 *(Evening devotions)*
10:30 p.m.—Psalm 139:8 *(Preparation for bed)*
11:00 p.m.—Psalm 4:4 *(Lights out)*

Herbert E. Saunders

Affirmation Booklets

Before your next retreat, assemble the following materials: colored paper, pens, pencils, markers, crayons, magazines, scissors, staplers and staples, glue, tape, and yarn. Then write the names of all the retreat participants (including the advisors) on slips of paper. On the first day of the event, have each person draw a name. The name you draw becomes your secret friend for the weekend.

Using the materials assembled, each person makes an Affirmation Booklet during the retreat, filling it with pictures, drawings, poems, Bible verses, and comments that will tell the secret friend what you have learned about her. This can include what you like or admire about the person, what talents you recognize, what you think the person con-

tributes to the group, what you miss most about her when she is not around—anything that will affirm your secret friend. One goal is to keep your secret friend a secret, trying to get to know that person without getting caught (so you must get to know several people in the process).

At the end of the retreat, gather everyone together for a prayer service, with time set aside to share the booklets. Present them one at a time so that all can enjoy watching the recipients reading their booklets. When you receive your booklet, it's your turn next to present the one you made. Close the prayer service with a familiar song.

Mary Kay Fitzpatrick

The Retreat Beatitudes

As your group leaves to go on its next retreat, have copies of the Retreat Beatitudes on page 33 ready to distribute to all youths and advisors. Post a copy as well in each cabin for the weekend. *Dave Carver*

Staff Auction

Here's a good camp activity the kids will enjoy. Ahead of time, ask everyone on the camp staff to donate a talent or service that can be auctioned

off. Make certain that all staff members are agreeable with whatever ideas you have. Also make sure

The Retreat Beatitudes

Blessed is the boy who remaineth in the boy's cabin, and also the boy who goeth not into the private rooms of the girl's cabin, for he shall live long and prosper. He shall also be allowed to remain here all weekend. But a curse is on those who find themselves in the wrong cabin; yea, both male and female shall remain in their appointed places.

Blessed are the young who are on time for meals, for they shall not be called washers of dishes.

Blessed are they who are called lovers of quiet, for they shall make many friends in the land. But a curse is on those who disturb others with thy radio or thy jam-box; and verily, I say unto thee, thy batteries may be taken if thou dost not heed a single warning to lower thy volume or stop thy tunes.

Blessed are they who pick up any trash they see, for the advisors shall smile upon them. But woe to those who go about leaving candy wrappers on the ground, and trash among the shrubs, for surely the cat-o'-nine-tails shall be applied to their hind-ends. And yea, this is no vain threat, but rather a promise of exceeding great surety.

Blessed are they who are known as high and dry this weekend, who avoid the creek, for they shall live to see their next birthday. But how terrible it will be for the one who falls into the cold, swirling waters of the deep, with no one to save him. It is better if that person had never been born.

Blessed are they who join with a whole heart in the games, songs, lessons, meals, and all that pertaineth to the retreat, for surely they shall be called "those who know how to have fun." Their fame shall spread throughout the land. But a curse of boredom will rest on those who playeth not our silly games.

that everyone is prepared to make good on offers of talent or service.

Here is a sample list:

• Sarah, dressed in a costume fit for a queen, will paddle you around the lake for an hour.
• Missy and Sean will take a cabin on a formal sunrise trail ride. (We are a horseback riding camp.)
• Mark will pop popcorn and serve it to a cabin around an evening campfire.
• John will take a cabin out of camp for an ice cream cone.
• Karen, Ron, and Kim will dress a cabin up as entertainers and sing with them at Sunday dinner.
• Cathy is willing to serve breakfast in bed for whichever cabin can pay the price.
• Julie and Kelly will serve a candlelight dinner to a cabin, complete with formal dress and flowers on the table.
• Cindy, Erica, and Jose will serenade a cabin with selected songs from our songbook, then tuck the cabin members in bed at night.
• Joe and Linda, our lifeguards, will provide a nighttime splash party for a cabin.
• Muriel will read bedtime stories from a book mutually acceptable to cabin and staff member.
• Joseph will plan a campout, complete with ghost stories.

At the auction, have the kids bid in cabin groups. Counselors can sit with their groups to help supervise the bidding. Appoint an auctioneer to handle the actual bidding. You will also need a bookkeeper to keep track of the money spent and purchases made.

Each cabin should be given an equal amount of camp dollars or play money to bid with. If you're raising funds for a project, use real money.

If you make sure that all the items on the list appeal to the campers, this will be a howling success! *Eileen Thompson*

PROGRAMMING

FRIENDSHIP CANDLE

Lighting a friendship candle is a good way to begin a retreat or camp. Get a candle that will last the length of the event. When your group is first assembled, have one person light it and place it where it will be seen frequently by everyone. Then explain that the candle is to be a reminder of the many warm friendships you're making while you're together.

On the last night of the event, have the group form a circle with small candles of their own. From the flame of the friendship candle, light one of the smaller candles and then pass on the light. Close with remarks such as these: "The warmth and light of the friendships that were made here will remain with us no matter how many miles come between us. So we no longer need the flame of our friendship candle, because the flame is now in our hearts."

Then blow out the friendship candle and end with prayer or a song. *Jan Schaible*

FAMILY COMMUNION

This can be a meaningful experience for families in a family retreat setting. Following a service emphasizing the family and the importance of family devotions, allow each family to have Communion together as a family unit. Give the fathers the elements of Communion and the mothers a candle. Each family then finds a place around the camp area to share Scripture and Communion together. After about 15 minutes all the families meet for a closing campfire service. The fathers can together light the campfire with their family's candle. *Chester P. Jenkins*

CATACOMB CHRISTIANS

Here's an idea that would work well during the night at a lock-in or retreat. Blindfold your kids and take them to a mystery location—preferably a dark, musty basement or cave. The only light should be from candles. Once inside, the blindfolds can be removed. Ask the kids to remain quiet. Your adult leaders should dress in early-Christian garb or in grubby clothes to indicate a life of hardship and suffering.

If you cannot locate a place that looks like a cave or catacombs, then find a place that feels like one and keep the blindfolds on the kids throughout the entire experience.

After you've arrived, read or recite from memory

the narration on page 36. Adapt it to your situation as you see fit.

After a time of sharing and singing, blindfold the kids again and take them back to church or your original location. Again ask them to be quiet as they leave. After they return, you can discuss the experience with them—how they felt, what they learned, what they would have done at the time, etc. *Denny Finnegan*

Personal Trees

Sometimes teens need to be enticed away from close friends during retreats in order to hear the Lord. A creative way to do this is to assign each group member a personal tree or similar quiet-time spot. Explain beforehand, of course, your rationale—not to arbitrarily split up friends, but to provide for them the opportunity that they probably wouldn't make for themselves otherwise—to hear God and meditate on his Word.

You can make it interesting by arranging for the day's schedule or the morning reading or other secret orders to be nailed to each tree when your kids arrive at them in the morning, or even for secret-pal gift distribution, etc.

A variation of this idea is to allow each camper time to select a personal tree in the area and stake it out. They may hang their name on it with a piece of paper and a thumbtack. Each day the kids go to their tree at a designated time for personal devotions. This tree remains their tree throughout the duration of the camp for quiet times or meditation. Some mini-messages given by the camp leadership preceding the devotional time can be centered around trees in the Bible (e.g., Zaccheus and the Sycamore tree, The Garden of Eden, The Tree of Life, the tree on which Christ was crucified, etc.). The actual text can then be studied by the campers individually. *Michael W. Capps and Frederick H. Schaffner*

Coffeehouse at Camp

A great activity for a night at camp is to have a coffeehouse program. Divide the campers into groups of about seven each at the beginning of the camp. Ask each group to develop a coffeehouse presentation such as drama, singing, reading, etc.

During the evening, each group will have the opportunity to make its presentation.

Set up for the coffeehouse by covering the tables with white paper. If the tables can be folded, lie them on the floor in a shape of a circle. Have the campers bring their sleeping bags and blankets to sit or lie upon in front of the tables. Use candles on the tables for light. Have Russian tea, donuts, and popcorn for refreshments. Begin with singing and guitar music. Let each group make its presentation. Close with a time of sharing and prayer. *William C. Moore*

Hike in the Woods

Divide the group into smaller groups of six to eight and give each of these groups a large paper bag. The groups are to stay separate. Send them on a hike for a half hour or an hour. Tell them they may pick up anything they wish and put the items in the paper bag: litter, rocks, leaves, flowers, grasses, etc. Now tell each group to create something out of what they have collected, but the rocks can't be rocks, litter can't be litter, etc. Possibilities might include a castle, a zoo, an animal (with leaves for ears), or a stereo system (with "rock" albums). Have each group see what the others did while construction is explained. *Senior High Fellowship, First Congregational Church*

Identify the Sound

Divide into groups of about six people each. Give each group a cassette tape recorder and ask them to go into a secluded part of the forest and tape three minutes of nature sounds. Each group should record on paper the identity of each sound. After each group has returned, the cassettes may be exchanged and each group will have a different recording to identify. Give each group five minutes to identify as many sounds as possible. The group that identifies the most is the winner. *William C. Moore*

Vice Versa

This activity motivates people to memorize Scripture and is especially useful at retreats. Assign different verses to each small group. However, point out that small groups are to memorize the

CATACOMB CHRISTIANS

The first-century Christians of Rome used to meet in catacombs—underground tunnels where they buried people. Now it may seem a strange place to meet, but there was a good reason for it. At that time it was illegal for people *not* to worship Caesar. And Christians felt they could worship *only* Jesus. If they were willing to worship Caesar as well, then they would have been officially tolerated—but those Christians just couldn't.

So the arrests and persecution began—and the punishment for not worshipping Caesar was death. The Romans had several methods for executing these Christians, these followers of a new Jewish cult called "The Way." At first they pitted them against gladiators, but these fool Christians refused to fight back. So in order to give the crowds more entertainment (Roman spectators paid to watch these spectacles), they released wild, half-starved beasts on them. Often Christians would be tied into the skins of freshly slaughtered cattle or deer in order to attract the fierce attacks of wild dogs—who'd rip them apart. For more entertainment, they'd saturate Christians with oil, coat them with flammable flax, and ignite them as human torches to illuminate nighttime entertainment in the arena. You could hear their screams, but they were soon drowned out by the crowd's screams of delight.

It became common to see roads lined with crucified bodies—some struggling to live, some struggling to die. And the crime posted on their crosses read something like "Seditionist—Christian."

That's why we started hiding in these catacombs—so we could continue worshipping our Jesus, the only true God. We began making secret signs so we could identify one another. For example, one of us would draw a straight line in the dirt; when another Christian noticed it, he'd cross it with another straight line, forming a cross. Or one would draw a short curved line, and another—with a similar stroke—would form a simple fish. That really confused the Romans because they didn't know what it meant—at first. You see, the letters in the Greek word *fish (ichthus)* were the first letters of the words in the Greek phrase for "Jesus Christ, God's Son, Savior."

But driven to secrecy made it easier for people to misunderstand us. They said we consumed human flesh and blood—barbarians with a ritual of human sacrifice. But they didn't understand that we were only celebrating our Lord's supper, his last one, with bread and wine and a common meal. The bread represented his body—broken on the cross—and wine represented his blood—shed on the cross, both of which he gave for our sins. They also represented our willingness to die for Jesus.

But rumors spread. Soon they were accusing us of all sorts of crimes. I guess it made it easier for them to do what they did to us in the arena and on the roads. When Rome burned, that madman Nero used us Christians as scapegoats—when he may well have encouraged the arson himself. So much bloodshed for so many evil lies. Since just witnessing would often cost us our lives, we began to be called martyrs—Christians who knew that witnessing would mean death.

[Remove blindfolds now; have only candles for light]

As the Apostle Paul said in Romans 10:9, "If you confess with your mouth Jesus as Lord, and believe in your heart that God raised Him from the dead, you shall be saved." (NASB)

To confess Jesus as Lord meant that Caesar wasn't Lord—which was to sign your death warrant. Yet these early followers of the Christ did confess so, because they believed that Jesus would raise them from the dead, just as he is risen. He promises this to all his followers.

And when they would gather together, they'd share and sing of Jesus Christ. And as the Apostle instructed in Colossians 3:16, "Let the word of Christ richly dwell within you; with all wisdom teaching and admonishing one another with psalms and hymns and spiritual songs, singing with thankfulness in your hearts to God." (NASB)

Let's do some of that now—share Scripture and songs with one another.

verses that have been given to other small groups, not their own. They should learn as many verses as possible to earn the most points. You decide how to award points.

To stimulate their desire to memorize, have kids write out verses to hang on doors and beds, and even print them on toilet paper, etc. Finally, have kids write down verses from memory. Give prizes to the individual and the team that memorizes the most verses. Most likely, kids will know the verses by memory six months later. *Kathy Neese*

NATURE SPEAKS

Each youth is asked to take a walk through the woods, around a lake, or around a camp setting. The purpose of this walk is to select an object from the environment that best expresses how they are feeling right now. Afterwards, in a group activity, teens ask others what that object reveals about them. Youths may, if they wish, explain how their selections "spoke" to them. *Timothy J. Mann*

MATURITY HUNT

At a camp, retreat, or lock-in where students can observe each other and their leaders over a period of time, do a lesson on Christian maturity. Following the study, give students a copy of Maturity Hunt on page 38, listing several descriptions of maturity. Their assignment: to be on the lookout for examples of each description in the behavior of other people. After a designated time for observation, discuss the results. *Ed Laremore*

RETREAT WORSHIP

In a natural setting, such as an outdoor amphitheater, give each youth a card with the following instructions for an alone time. Attached to the card are three pipe cleaners. Have them go off by themselves for a period of time and do the following:
Instructions:
1. Take pipe cleaners and think about a relationship with God. Put them together in some way that would express symbolically that relationship with him.
2. Think about these areas of your relationship:

—What kind of relationship do I have?
—How can I better it?
—Do I only look to him when I'm in a rut or have a problem, or do I talk with him daily?
—Christian, that's what I'm called, but what does that mean to me?
—How do I share Christ with my friends, honestly?
—Am I hanging around the right people?
—How do my friends influence me in my decisions?
—Do I really love my friends?
—What does Christian love mean to me?
3. Take your Bible and read the passage found in 2 Corinthians 5:14, 15, 17 (it may also be printed on the other side of the card).
4. At a given signal, come back to a central place and share pipe cleaner symbols with several other persons or with the total group, and some other feelings about the experience.
Jean Parker

HUMANS WERE HERE!

Divide into groups of six to eight campers and give each group a large bag. Tell the groups they are to find as many signs of people (litter, cans, cigarette butts, etc.) as they can within a given time limit. The group that collects the most is the winner. This is an effective way to clean up an area. It also leads into a significant discussion on the effect people have had on the environment. *William C. Moore*

SKI-TRIP AFFIRMATION

This worksheet provides a good community builder for use during a ski retreat. Distribute copies of page 39 and have kids fill it out. Follow up with an affirmation bombardment in which kids explain their choices listed on the sheet. *George T. Warren*

HOLY LIFT TICKETS

Ski trips are notorious for being fun but spiritually unproductive times for many youth groups. In order to get enough runs for the cost of the lift ticket, skiers usually go from the opening of the lift to closing time with barely a stop for food, much less

MATURITY HUNT

What does spiritual maturity look like?

The following statements exemplify several aspects of maturity. During our time together notice people around you whose behavior illustrates these different aspects of spiritual maturity. When you observe someone living out one of the marks of maturity, summarize the incident in the box next to the description, and then ask the person you observed to initial the appropriate box. You may also list incidents that violate the different aspects. Record those incidents in the appropriate boxes as well. No initials are needed in these cases!

What maturity is	Circumstances surrounding the mature behavior I observed	Initial
1. Maturity is the ability to control anger and settle differences without violence or destruction.		
2. Maturity is patience—the willingness to pass up immediate pleasure in favor of long-term gain.		
3. Maturity is perseverance—the ability to sweat out a project or a situation in spite of opposition and discouraging setbacks.		
4. Maturity is unselfishness—responding to the needs of others, often at the expense of one's own desires or wishes.		
5. Maturity is the capacity to face unpleasantness and frustration, discomfort and defeat, without complaint or collapse.		
6. Maturity is humility. It is being big enough to say, "I was wrong." And when right the mature person need not say, "I told you so."		
7. Maturity is the ability to make a decision and stand by it. The immature spend their lives exploring endless possibilities and achieving nothing.		
8. Maturity means dependability, keeping one's word, coming through in a crisis. The immature—confused and disorganized—are masters of the alibi. Their lives are a maze of broken promises, former friends, unfinished business, and good intentions that never materialize.		
9. Maturity is the art of living in peace with that which we cannot change.		
10. Maturity is knowing how to give and receive love.		
11. Maturity is the ability to learn from experience.		

SKi-TRip AFFiRMATION

Place the initials or first name of someone in your group next to the statement that best describes that person. Make sure you find a statement for each person in your group (or add your own ski-related statements at the end). Double up or triple up on names per line if needed.

_____1. Trail Signs—You show me the way.

_____2. Ski Partner—I enjoy your company.

_____3. A New Snow—You're a chance for a new start.

_____4. Chair Lift—You give me a lift!

_____5. Mogul—You're a challenge that strengthens me.

_____6. Beginner's Slope—I feel comfortable and secure around you.

_____7. Skis—You help me keep going.

_____8. Ski Boots—You keep me stable; protect me.

_____9. Trees—You make the trip beautiful.

_____10. Long Underwear—You are not obvious, but needed!

_____11. Poles—You help me up when I fall/fail.

_____12. Parka—You protect me from the bitterness around me.

_____13. Goggles—You help me see when it's hard to see.

_____14. Mountain Stream—You are refreshing, cool.

_____15. Ski Patrol—You are always there when I need you.

_____16. Other _____.

time for devotions or Bible study.

To help students reflect on God's creation, hand out daily Holy Lift Tickets (page 41) for one day's reflection. Blanks are included for you to insert your own verses and reflections for the other days of your trip. It's not only a fun activity for your kids, but also a meaningful one. *Eugene C. Scott*

BIRTHDAYS AT CAMP

Most junior high kids enjoy celebrating their birthdays, and this idea will make it possible for all the kids to celebrate their birthdays at camp instead of only a select few. Designate each day as representing two months of the year (such as Monday for January and February, Tuesday for March and April, etc.) A six-day camp would cover the whole year. Then each day, celebrate the birthdays of the kids whose birthdays fall in the corresponding two months. Sing the happy birthday song, give small novelty gifts for presents, and grant each day's birthday kids certain special privileges. *William Moore*

NO COUNSELOR—NO BREAKFAST

During a week-long camp, it is often a lot of fun to have an early morning counselor hunt. Have all the counselors wake up before their campers and then find places to hide within a specified area. The campers are then awakened to the announcements that they must first find their counselor before they can have breakfast. *William Moore*

BIBLE PICTURE POSTERS

This can be a creative and stimulating activity for a camp, weekend retreat, or all-day outing. Begin with a Bible study and divide into small groups of four or five. Then give each group a Polaroid camera and a roll or two of film. Have the kids go out and shoot a series of pictures that illustrate either the portion of Scripture studied or another of their own choosing. After the pictures are completed, provide poster board, magic markers, tape, etc., and have the groups create posters using their pictures, the Scripture, and their own creativity. The posters are then placed on display and can be enjoyed by everyone. *Lavern Kruse*

HANDMADE GIFTS

This is a good idea for camps or weekend retreats. At the beginning of camp, have each kid draw a name from a box containing everyone's name written on a slip of paper. Then ask the kids to create a gift for the person whose name they drew. The gift should be completed by the end of camp or some other specified time. Materials can be provided such as glue, paints, pieces of wood, metal, string, etc. The gifts can be made of anything, but should be made with that special person in mind. No one should reveal who they are making their gift for until the time when the gifts are exchanged. Follow up with a discussion on giving and receiving, or on the meaning of the various gifts that were created. *James Allard*

MYSTERY PERSONALITIES

Here's a great way to add a little mystery to your next camp or retreat. Select three persons to be Mystery Personalities and at each meal, give out clues to their identity. Campers then try to solve the mystery by putting together the clues and asking a lot of questions. The fist person to correctly guess the identities of all three wins a prize (or points for her team, etc.). The three Mystery Personalities can be people at camp or famous people (such as Bible characters) that the kids would know. Don't make the clues too easy. Make them tough. As the camp nears its end, the clues can be made easier if no one has been able to guess correctly. *Curt Finch*

RAID REGULATION

Nearly every junior and senior high camp or retreat will include one or more raids in which a full-scale water balloon war breaks out in and around the cabins, usually in the middle of the night. Sometimes these raids can get completely out of hand. One good way to tame them down is to simply plan the notorious raid right into the camp schedule, perhaps on a Friday night. On the first day of camp, give each kid a water balloon (or two) attached to a card explaining the rules, boundaries, and time limits for the raid. Thus, everyone in the

HOLY LIFT TICKET

This ticket entitles bearer to time with God.

Good only on _____

"A cheerful heart is good medicine, but a crushed spirit dries up the bones." (Proverbs 17:22)

For at least today, don't picture God as some cosmic cop, eager to lock us up or knock us over the head whenever we stray dangerously close to having fun. Look around you...God's creation is amazing. He must have enjoyed himself immensely when he invented mountains and snow. The stroke of genius, though, was creating in us the ability to enjoy his mountains and snow.

So take advantage of God's creation today. Ski, laugh, hang out with your friends. And sometime—maybe even right now—say a simple prayer of thanks for all the good things God has given you.

HOLY LIFT TICKET

This ticket entitles bearer to time with God.

Good only on _____

HOLY LIFT TICKET

This ticket entitles bearer to time with God.

Good only on _____

camp is involved, preventing only a few kids from having fun at the expense of others. It's also much easier than trying to squelch the inevitable. *Luke Harkey*

ROTATE

This camp activity is ideal for wet weather, especially when it has been raining for several days, and there is nothing but mud and wetness all around. It's also good when you don't have a large indoor room for games and activities on rainy days. The campers are divided into small groups of anywhere from 10 to 25 kids each, depending on your situation. Cabins are cleared as much as possible of debris, and beds are arranged so that there is room for kids to move around. Campers are instructed to dress for rain and wear old clothes under rain gear. In each cabin, one staff member conducts an activity. Use your imagination for this. Games like Killer, Charades, simulation games, crafts, movies, singing, etc., are all possibilities. Every 40 minutes or so, each group rotates to a new cabin and a new activity. The leaders stay put with the same activity for the new group. This can continue until each group has experienced each activity. It really helps prevent boredom on those dreary days. *Louie Vesser*

YOUR LOVING OFFSPRING

Most kids don't bother to write home while at summer camp, so here's a solution to that problem. Distribute copies of page 43 and have all of the kids fill it out. Provide envelopes and postage, and mail them out early in the week. Parents do enjoy hearing from their kids, and this is a fun way to get it done. *Bill Vestal*

COMMITMENT LOG

If your camp has been designed for a campfire commitment service at the end of the week, here is a great way to dramatize each individual's choice and course of action. Stand a log about three feet tall behind a bale of hay within the campfire circle. The log should be able to stand up by itself. The top of the log should be cut at a 45 degree angle and sanded so that people can write on it.

At the conclusion of the commitment service, invite the kids to kneel on the bale of hay and sign their names on the angled end of the log with a

felt-tip pen. Encourage all the campers to take some time in prayer about the commitment they wish to make. And by proper explanation try to avoid a lineup at the hay bale and log altar. When all have had a chance to sign their names, insert the inscribed end of the log into the fire as an offering to God and close with prayer. *Barry DeShetler*

COUNSELOR FASHION SHOW

Have cabin groups at camp compete to see which one can dress up their counselor in the most outrageous outfit. They can use anything they want for clothes and accessories. The youths will really enjoy this, and the results are a lot of laughs. Set a time limit for the dress up period, and offer a prize (or points if you have competition) for the funniest, ugliest, most unique, etc. *Shirley Raferson*

HOLY GROUND

To enhance the personal devotions of kids at camp, have them go out on the first day by themselves and select a private area that is about one square yard. They can mark this area anyway they want (with rocks, branches, or whatever). This is to be their own little plot of holy ground for the entire week.

Each day the students are given instructions for their personal devotions in the morning, and they go to their holy ground where God will meet them. You might want to introduce this by reading the passage from the Old Testament about Moses and

Letter from Camp

(Circle the best answer.)

Dear (a) folks (b) Sir (c) Ms. (d) Mommy and Daddy (e)_____:

I am feeling (a) miserable (b) hungry (c) despondent (d) great (e) so-so (f) sick (g) lower than a snake's belly (h) as well as can be expected after breaking my leg (i)_____.

My financial condition is (a) zero (b) fine after I ripped off my counselor's wallet (c) okay (d) dependent on how fast you can send me some bread (e) I'm loaded (f)_____.

I will come home when (a) I run out of money (b) I feel like it (c) the sun refuses to come up in the morning (d) you promise to be nice to my new pet rattlesnake (e)_____.

I sleep a lot here because (a) I'm lazy (b) I like to save wear and tear on my clothes (c) I'm into energy conservation (d)_____.

My spiritual life is (a) angelic (b) great (c) at low ebb (d) up and down (e)_____.

Most of my friends here are (a) guys (b) girls (c) squirrels (d) in trouble since they met me (e) not too bright (f) fine (g)_____.

Camp food is (a) rotten (b) okay (c) great (d) rationed (e) no nutritional value (f) fine, if you have an iron stomach (g)_____.

Yesterday I learned that (a) 2 and 2 make 4 (b) they'll send me home if I don't shape up (c) you moved (d) there's no such thing as Santa Claus (e) it hurts when you fall from a 50-foot-high cliff (f)_____.

I have decided (a) to get married while I'm up here (b) that camps are for the birds (c) to join a rock and roll band (d)_____.

There isn't much else to say except: _____ — _____.

Your loving offspring,

_____

(signed)

the burning bush: "Take your shoes off, Moses, for you are on holy ground." The kids might even want to remove their shoes each day as they have their time alone with God. At first campers might not be too impressed with this idea, but as the days pass, many youths will be spending more and more time at their holy ground alone with God. It can become a very special place.

To help the kids continue this when they go home, give each camper a small jar, and have them dig up some of their holy ground to take home as a reminder to spend some time alone with God every day. *Gary Fulfer*

LETTER FROM CAMP

Explain that you intercepted this letter at the camp post office. Announce that letters like this are not allowed. Work the names of some of the kids at camp into the letter to make it more fun.

> Dear _____,
> My week at camp is just about over. _____ is a nice place to camp—30-million mosquitoes can't be wrong.
> The brochure claimed that every room overlooked a beautiful canyon. They also overlooked indoor toilets, mattresses, and running water. My room is so small that the mice are hunchbacked. It does have a nice bath . . . I'd rather have a bed.
> The cabin is modern. It has chrome doorknobs, chrome banisters, and chrome windowsills. As a matter of fact, its the chromiest room I've ever been in.
> Really, this is the place for mosquitoes. It's getting so you don't want to swat any of them because you don't want to kill your own flesh and blood.
> We got up early and went water-skiing on the lake this morning. First time I ever went. I got behind the boat and up on the skis with the line in my hand until one ski went one way and the other went the other way and [chuckle] . . . I thought I'd split! While I was recuperating, the camp nurse, Heather, told me to drink a glass of warm milk after a hot bath. Silly nurse, I couldn't even finish drinking the hot bath.
> Love, _____

THE JOURNEYS OF PAUL

Sometimes certain passages of Scripture can be made to come alive for young people by recreating them in a modern setting. The missionary journeys of Paul lend themselves well to this, especially if you have access to a camp or retreat facility where there is plenty of room and a body of water, like a lake.

Before the teens arrive, set everything up. Get a map of Paul's journeys and lay everything out. Put up some signs that mark the locations of appropri-

ate towns, countries, etc. Existing buildings or landmarks can be made to be anything you want them to be. Use any props that you think might help. The nice thing about a camp is that you can make anything be whatever you want it to be.

When the group arrives, explain to them that they are about to go on a missionary journey with Paul. As you progress through the cities and countries, stop at each one and read or tell what Paul did there or what happened to him. You could even act some of these out if possible. If Paul walked, then you walk. If he had to travel by boat, then have the kids travel in boats. It can be a very effective way to make the Scriptures come to life. *Aaron Bell*

MEDITATION TRAIL

Here's a great devotional idea for small groups on a retreat. With some adaptation, it could be used with larger groups. It will work best in a large camp area or wilderness where there is plenty of room to spread out.

Prior to the event, a trail is set up all over the camp, with various places marked along the way as stop points or meditation points. The trail should be clearly marked and should form a large circle so that it begins and ends at the same place, if possible.

Each participant is given an envelope in which they will find several slips of paper, the same number as there are stop points along the train. Each piece of paper has a Bible verse and a suggestion for

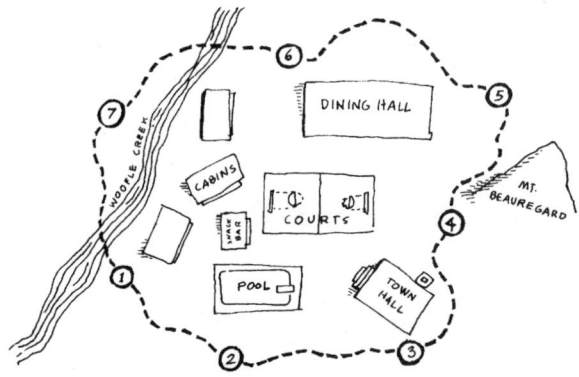

meditation, numbered in the order that they should be used. The students are then sent off on the trail one by one at five-minute intervals. As they come to a stop point, they take out the appropriate meditation from the envelope and read it, spending two or three minutes meditating on the thought provided.

The walk should be done without talking or other unnecessary noise or activity. Of course, if everyone cooperates, there will be no other persons close enough for conversation.

If you want to send the group out all at once, then send each person to a different stop point for their first meditation. There will then be one person at each point to begin, and they can just move along until they have stopped at all of them. Use a whistle to indicate each five minute interval when everyone should move on to the next point.

Another variation would be to simply post a meditation at each stop point, rather than giving each person an envelope. However you use this idea, you can be sure that kids will enjoy this new approach to devotions and Bible study at camp. *David Baumann*

WILDERNESS WORSHIP CENTER

Many retreats will conclude with a worship service on Sunday morning. A great way for a group to create their own place for this worship service is to find an open area around the camp somewhere that is surrounded by trees or posts. Take a roll of good strong rope, cord, or wire, and wrap it around the

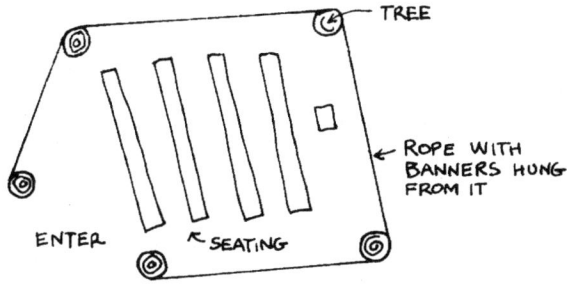

TREE

ROPE WITH BANNERS HUNG FROM IT

ENTER   SEATING

area about four or five feet above the ground. It doesn't have to be a perfect square.

On the day before the worship service, have all the campers make banners or posters on a common theme or on anything they want. Then prior to the worship service, have campers hang their banners and posters on the line around the worship area.

Depending on the location, you can provide chairs or logs for seating, or kids can sit on the ground. The worship will have added meaning since the campers have actually created their own church for the service. *Chuck Campbell*

SECRET PALS

This is a good community-building exercise for your next camp or retreat. At the beginning of the week or weekend, have everyone write their names on little slips of paper. Place all the names in a box, and have everyone draw a name (not their own). This name is to be their secret pal throughout the camp or retreat. They are instructed to perform small acts of friendship for their secret pal, but always doing it in secret, so that they won't know who is responsible. For example, kids might send their secret pal a bouquet of flowers, a love letter, a box of candy, or arrange for them not to have to do K.P.

At the end of the experience, the veil of secrecy can be removed, and usually the results are very good. Some lasting friendships can get started this way. *Gail Moody*

SURPRISE PACKAGES FROM HOME

Most kids love to get something in the mail when they are away at camp. It can be quite disappointing for campers when they hope they will get something, but nothing ever comes. To remedy this, secretly contact all the parents of the campers in advance, and ask them to prepare a surprise package for their child. These can be collected without the youths knowing anything about them, and then, on whatever day you choose, they can all be handed out at once. The kids will freak out. You might want to specify to the parents the type of thing that would be best in the package, but let each parent give whatever they want. It would also be a good idea to take a few extras, just in case.

A good variation of this, with perhaps a lot more meaning, would be to have a session at camp on self-worth, or on talents, gifts, abilities, and the like. During the session, teens can get into small groups, and do a type of self-evaluation, asking themselves questions like "What are my strengths?

What are my abilities and how can I best use them?" Then, toward the conclusion of this session, surprise packages can be produced from each camper's parents, with a note from the parents affirming the strengths and special abilities of their child. The gift in the package can be symbolic of the gifts that the child brings to the family. Again, these surprise packages should be collected and stashed away without the kids knowing anything about them. The students can then share these gifts with each other if they want. The results of something like this can be very effective.

Dennis McDonough

THE BOARD OF DESTINY

Every church camp in the world has had a rule for at least a hundred years that if a camper gets a package or three letters at mail call, he or she must tell a joke or sing a song to get the mail. This idea could be used in similar circumstances.

The Board of Destiny is a poster board with about 50 little doors cut into it (like an Advent calendar). Behind each door is a message that can be either good news or bad news for the one who opens it. Messages might include:
• The camp dean buys you a can of soda at the canteen.
• Go to the front of the line for your next meal.
• The faculty member of your choice serves you a meal.
• You are exempted from cabin cleanup tomorrow.
   However, some of the messages might say:
• Do 10 push-ups.
• You must buy the camp dean a can of soda from the canteen.
• You are sentenced to 10 seconds in front of the firing squad (squirt guns).
• Eat your next meal without a chair.

One section of the board can be called Heaven on Earth, and these doors are opened only by people who deserve some special award. This section might include these messages:
• You have priority on the diving board for one day.
• You can be the firing squad for the counselor of your choice.
• You get a free ice cream sundae at the canteen.

The board can also feature Death Row, which is for kids who deserve something more negative. This could be used in a creative way to handle discipline problems. Messages in this section might include:
• Wipe off all the tables.
• Sweep the dining hall.
• You're last in line at the next meal.
• Carry all the dishes from all the tables.
• You must be a staff gofer for the rest of the day.

You can use all these messages or others of your choosing. This idea will add a little excitement at mail call and other fun times. Use it creatively. It's great fun and has a variety of applications. *Rod Nielsen*

CONVERSATION SHEETS

Here's a great way for kids to engage in dialogue with each other at a camp or retreat in a non-threatening way. Get a roll of butcher paper about four feet wide, and roll it out on a couple of tables or hang it on the wall. Provide pencils and markers and then encourage your kids to write down their feelings and comments as the week goes by. Don't limit what they write about (although they usually will want to write about things that are happening on the retreat). Tell them they can sign their names if they want, but they don't have to.

Then encourage the kids to read the comments and respond to them if they want to. You'll be amazed at how much the kids will help each other. Here is an actual sample from a conversation sheet used at one camp:

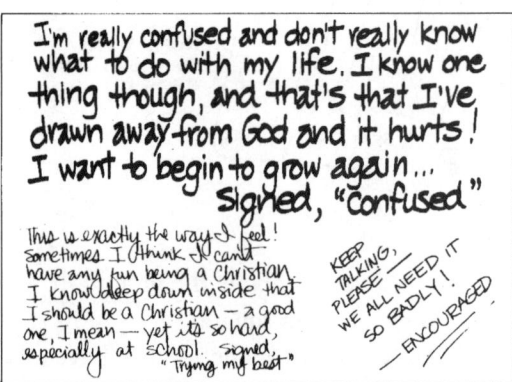

Kids can write things that are just for fun as well. Either way, it provides an outlet for some creativity and serious thinking. By reading these conversation sheets, your leaders can also get a good feel for what's happening in your group. Make sure it's located in a prominent place where kids will see it often. *Jim Roberts*

RETREAT FOLDERS

Keep your youth in suspense on a retreat by revealing the weekend's agenda only one item at a time. Issue folders at the beginning, to which are added instructions, schedules, and other information page-by-page throughout the weekend. The kids can decorate the materials however they like. If you use folders with page clamps, they can be kept as a permanent keepsake of the retreat. *David Johnson*

COMIN' DOWN FROM THE MOUNTAIN

It's not unusual for some kids to worry about what will happen to them when they return home from a camp, retreat, or mission trip—especially if it was a meaningful, spiritual experience for them. To help your kids deal with those fears, invite them to write their fears on paper and turn them in at the last meeting. They will probably include such things as "school pressures," "not being able to explain what happened," "still being faithful to God," "getting along with my non-Christian parents," and so on.

After these have been turned in, you can read them and share some thoughts from Scripture to help the kids deal with their fears and specific problems, and as a group you can pray for each one. It would also be wise to plan follow-up experiences to support the kids and to help them remember their commitments. *Lee Strawhun*

DO-GOOD BUCKS

Here's the gist of this camping idea: a few months before camp, you call merchants around town and ask for tax-deductible donations of radios, stuffed animals, school supplies, gift certificates, tennis shoes, Bibles, books, records, candy bars, and other munchies—even a bicycle or two.

During camp week, kids earn Bonus Bucks (you print prior to camp) by doing something kind, good, or civil on their own initiative: picking up

trash, running errands, cleaning cabins, organizing Whenever counselors observe such meritorious behavior, they write up a receipt—on an actual

sales pad—listing the act and the number of Bonus Bucks that the counselor deems the act is worth (use increments of 1,000). Campers then cash in their receipts for Bonus Bucks.

A few hours before camp ends, conduct an auction for the donated merchandise, which kids pay for with their Bonus Bucks. Ideas like this can help make camp a cooperative, unified time of kids working with—not against—counselors. And it makes for a highly anticipated and exciting end-of-week, too! *Mike Gulotta*

HERE I RAISE MINE EBENEZER

Remember that line from the hymn "Come, Thou Fount of Every Blessing"? God instructed Israel to set up a stone to commemorate their defeat of the Philistines, and to call it Ebenezer—"stone of help" (1 Sam. 7:12). At other times, such as at the crossing of the Jordan River (Josh. 4:1-9), Israel would build a stone altar intended to memorialize the Lord's help.

Though your teens return from camp or a retreat in optimistic spirits, especially if God dealt decisively with them there, they'll need a reminder through the year of their deliverance. So with a bit of plan ning, they can make their own stone memorial that reminds them of the truth and power of what happened in them during the last summer.

The last day of camp, ask those who experienced significant spiritual deliverance of any sort to bring with them on the bus a fairly good-sized

rock—one they probably need both hands to lift, though not a backbreaker. When they arrive back at church, choose a site that is visible yet not in the mainstream—maybe a corner of your property—and stack your rocks into a memorial.

Since everyone will probably be too tired on the same day you return from camp, wait until the next Sunday afternoon or midweek meeting to hold a service. Gathered around your memorial, have some young people share what God accomplished in them during camp. Then read the Joshua 4 passage, explaining what a memorial symbolizes: a gravestone (a reminder of things past, things that God has dealt finally with), a signpost (a marker for good things currently underway, works that God began in them at camp), and a contract (a covenant of things to come—i.e., God will never abandon them, but will continue the work in them he started).

Close with communion—which is, in fact, another kind of altar. Refer to the memorial often throughout the year to remind the kids what God did, is doing, and will do in them. *Jon Davidson*

CONVICT COMMUNITY

Kids learn the definition of teamwork in a hurry with this exercise in togetherness. At your next retreat pair up kids by handcuffing them together with two-foot lengths of soft poly rope. Tie a bowline knot at each end. Members of each pair place one of their hands into the knot to become secured to their partners. (A bowline knot neither slips off nor restricts circulation.) As kids play games, eat meals, attend meetings, and go through their daily routines, ask them to consider their experience a parable about living one's life with others in mind.

Before the kids are tied together, explain safety precautions—move more slowly than normal, give advance warning about changes of direction, don't yank at each other, always be aware of your partner. Set ground rules about bathroom breaks and privacy. Stress safety over and over whenever the groups meet together. *Pat McGlone*

WINDING DOWN AT NIGHT

Settling down a cabin full of junior high teens for the night doesn't have to stump you any more. It's a fact that listening to stories actually decreases the heart and respiration rates in people, allowing them to relax.

So make the traditional cabin bedtime story do double time for your campers: tell stories from your

own life. Since part of the camping experience is the melding together of the campers' lives with their counselor, retelling humorous personal anec-dotes about yourself lets kids know who you are and what you are about. With a little bit of advance planning, you can make an easy transition to the more serious side of your life and finally drift off to sleep after praying together. *Kevin Turner*

STUFFED ANIMALS

Fifth and sixth graders are often anxious about being away from home for an entire week of summer camp. To help alleviate their anxiety, make it mandatory for them to bring their favorite stuffed animal to camp. (Many want to anyway!)

When campers arrive, their stuffed animals are immediately turned over to a designated counselor. The counselor privately takes all fuzzy friends to a room where each animal is given an award—fuzzi-est, most lovable, cuddliest, brightest eyes, most love-worn, most adorable, most huggable, snuggli-est, strangest, etc.

After the evening meal that night, set all the stuffed animals out in the meeting room. Hold up each one while reading off its award, and then have the kids guess who it belongs to. Throughout the week the young people will proudly and gladly sleep with their stuffed animals because everyone has one. *Carolyn Peters*

GO AHEAD AND LEAF

Sometime during your next camping trip or retreat weekend, send teens out for a nature walk. Ask them to look around and find a leaf that describes them to other people. When the teens return, have them explain why they picked their leaf. Read some Bible verses that talk about leaves, for exam-ple, Proverbs 11:28 and Psalm 1:1-3.

This simple activity can cover a host of themes including obedience, self-image, and similarities and differences as a family. *Laura Weller*

STAR SEARCH

Want an unusual but effective segue into a talk or devotional during your next camping trip or night hike? If you'll be far enough away from the city to have really dark night skies, take the Night Sky handouts on pages 50-51 along, and spend a few minutes during the day pointing out the most obvi-ous constellations as they appear on the sheet. You may want different students to memorize the shape of different constellations.

That night, find a site away from lights—a field, a hilltop, even a dark parking lot works—as long as your view of the sky is as large as possible from hori-zon to horizon. Now let kids find their constella-tions—and watch for the slow-moving satellites within an hour or two of sunset, and for meteors (shooting stars) that zip across a corner of the sky.

Many of the constellations reflect biblical charac-ters (Virgo suggests Mary, Leo suggests either Christ or the lion Samson killed), events (Gemini the Twins suggests the birth and lives of Jacob and Esau), and themes (Boötes suggests shepherding, Draco and Scorpio suggest Satan). Come with a little prepara-tion, and give your talk right out there under the stars, as you connect the constellations and the sto-ries behind them with biblical truths. *Doug Partin*

THIS IS MY LIFE!

This four-part exercise on self-esteem and relation-ships is ideal for retreats.

The first part involves filling out life cards. Ask each young person to write the following informa-tion on index cards of various colors:

Cherry: My hopes and dreams for the future.

Yellow: Something for which I am grateful.

Green: How I have made a difference in the world.

The second part is to have kids choose three character traits that they think best describe them-selves. They can choose from the list below if they want or add as many as they like.

Compassion	Sense of humor
Listening	Creativity
Trustworthiness	Humility
Loyalty	Forgiveness
Sympathy	Independence

The Night Sky

Constellation names in all capital letters; other names are star names.

SPRING

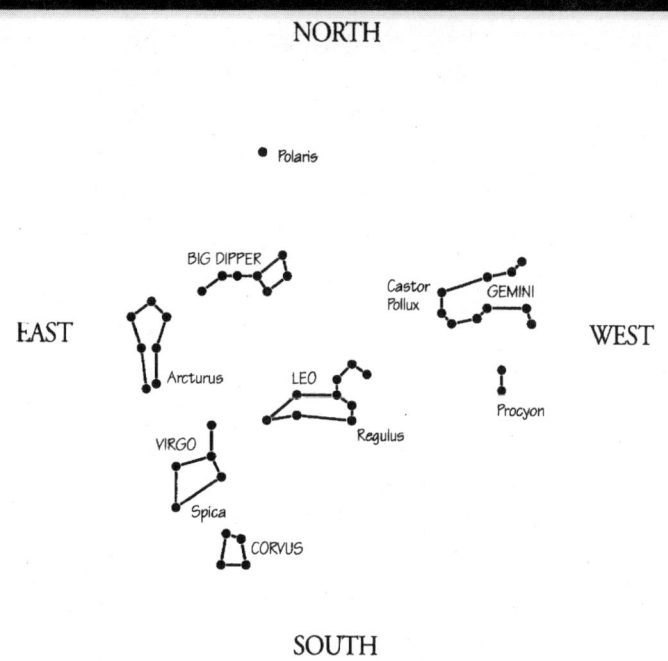

NORTH

• Polaris

BIG DIPPER

Castor
Pollux   GEMINI

EAST   WEST

Arcturus   LEO   Procyon

Regulus

VIRGO

Spica

CORVUS

SOUTH

• The handle of the **BIG DIPPER** "arcs to **Arcturus**."

• A line extended through the **BIG DIPPER**'s front two "pointer stars" takes you north to **Polaris**, the North Star, and the other way to **LEO** the Lion.

• The head of **LEO** the Lion is a big backwards question mark, with **LEO**'s brightest star, **Regulus**, at the bottom of the question mark.

SUMMER

• At the corners of the "Summer Triangle" are the brightest stars **Deneb**, **Vega**, and **Altair** (in **CYGNUS** the Swan, **LYRA** the Lyre, and **AQUILA** the Eagle, respectively).

• **CYGNUS** the Swan is also called the Northern Cross. The Swan flies south along the Milky Way.

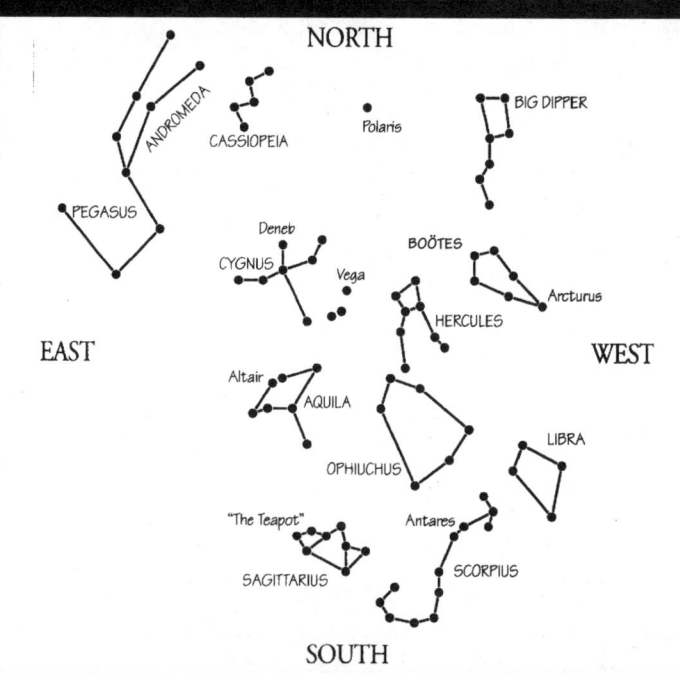

NORTH

ANDROMEDA   CASSIOPEIA   Polaris   BIG DIPPER

PEGASUS

Deneb   BOÖTES

CYGNUS   Vega   Arcturus

HERCULES

EAST   WEST

Altair   AQUILA   LIBRA

OPHIUCHUS

"The Teapot"   Antares

SAGITTARIUS   SCORPIUS

SOUTH

The Night Sky

AUTUMN

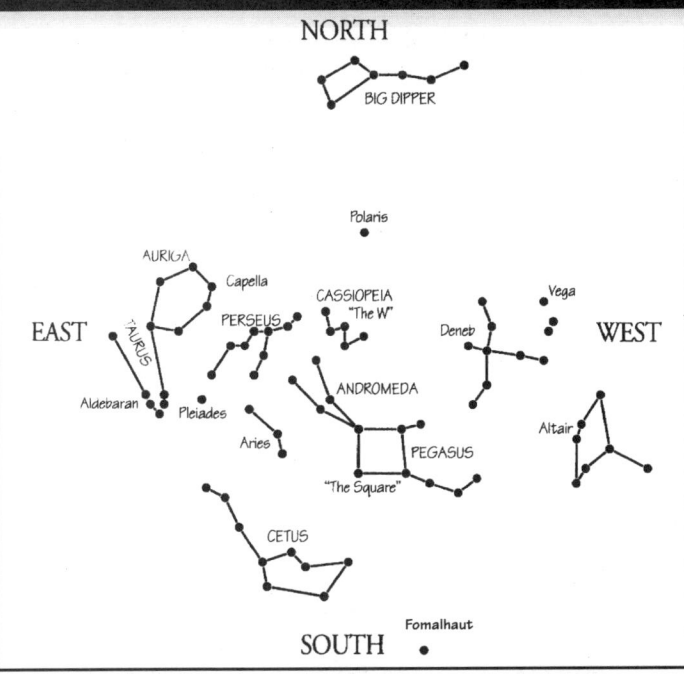

• High overhead is **CASSIOPEIA** the Queen, a "W" pattern of stars (some see an upside-down "M").

• The Great Square in the south is **PEGASUS** the Flying Horse.

• **CETUS** the Whale is in the south.

• **PERSEUS** is the hero who rescued **ANDROMEDA**, the daughter of **CASSIOPEIA** the Queen.

WINTER

• **ORION** the Hunter: The three closely spaced stars across the middle of **ORION** are his belt. A straight line drawn through the belt and extended to the right (and curved a little upward) brings you to Aldebaran, the reddish eye of **TAURUS** the Bull. Extended to the left, the line takes you to **Sirius**.

• Sirius: The "Dog Star," so named because it is the brightest star in **CANUS MAJOR**, the "Big Dog" of the hunter **ORION**. **Sirius** is also the brightest star in the night sky.

PLEIADES: A tiny "dipper" of jewel-like stars, to the northwest of **Aldebaran**.

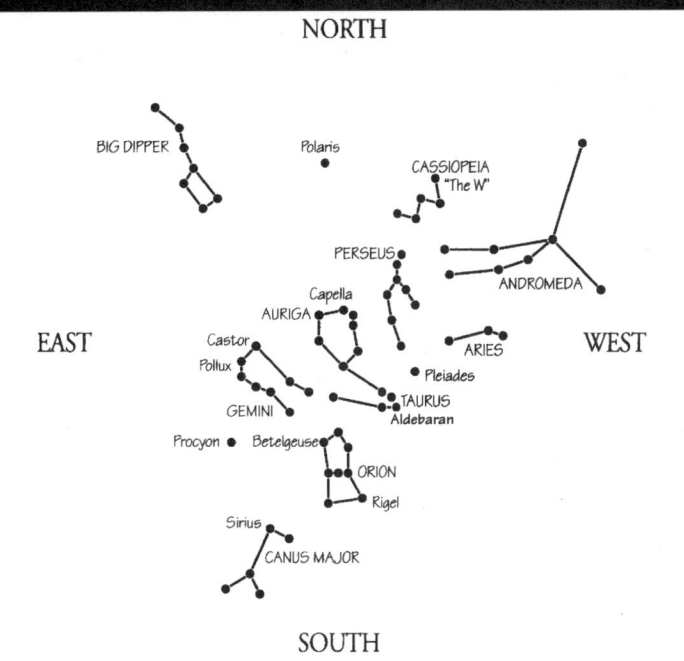

Obituary Notice 1

Imagine yourself a journalist who has to write an article on the person whose name and life cards you've been given. The object is to affirm this person, so use some imagination. Be kind—for someone's doing the same for you right now.

What is the person's name? **1** _____

List some of the activities that the person has been recently involved in (sports, drama, clubs, religious activities, hobbies, talents, etc.). Ask someone else (besides your subject) if you need help on this one.

2 _____

_____

Take a look at the person's character-trait list. How does this person see himself or herself?

3 _____

_____

Take a second look. How do others see this person?

4 _____

_____

Look at this person's green life card. What were things this person did, however small, that made a difference—things this person wants to be remembered for?

5 _____

_____

Who are some good friends of the person, especially in the group?

6 _____

_____

Find two people who know the person well, and get a quote from each of them about why they liked this person—especially what they liked inside the person—the inner, quiet qualities.

Friend's name: **7** _____

Friend's quote: **8** _____

Friend's name: **9** _____

Friend's quote: 10 _____

Look at your person's yellow life card. For what things is he or she grateful?

11 _____

Look at your person's cherry life card. What are the person's visions, hopes, and dreams for the future? **12** _____

_____

Write an outrageous noun here: **13** _____

Write the name of an organization in town here: **14** _____

Write a hobby or skill here: **15** _____

Write either a local or distant place of amusement here: **16** _____

Obituary Notice 2

1 _____ died yesterday on Elm Street. Details of the death are a mystery to everyone in the neighborhood. Word has is that the whole episode was a nightmare.

Recently involved in 2 _____, the deceased saw herself or himself as 3 _____ while others saw her or him as 4 _____.

General opinion is that she or he will be most remembered for 5 _____ _____. No one else could have done the same. She or he was persuaded that it is a wonderful life because of what she or he brought to it.

1 _____ will be missed by a number of folks, who, it turns out, are nearly crazed with grief: a Norman Bates (local hotel owner) is among them. Others who will miss her or him include 6 _____.

"8 _____," said 7 _____.

9 _____ added, "10 _____."

1 _____ was a thankful person, especially grateful for 11 _____. She or he had big plans ahead for herself or himself, plans that included 12 _____.

Instead of the customary flowers, 1 _____'s family and friends request that a donation of 13 _____ be given to her or his favorite charity, 14 _____, because of her or his great interest in 15 _____.

Funeral services will be held at 16 _____.

Caring Hopefulness
Cheerfulness Leadership
Helpfulness Optimism

The next step is to collect the kids' life cards and character-trait lists. Redistribute them so that each person has someone else's. They must then fill out Obituary Notice 1 on page 52 using information that they have, following the instructions on the sheet.

Lastly, the information is transferred to Obituary Notice 2 on page 53, number by number, which can then be returned to the "deceased" to be read either privately or aloud to the group.

This exercise is not only fun, but it's a good way for kids to affirm each other and to evaluate who they've become, what they're becoming, and what they hope to do and to be in the future. *Bruce Clanton*

MINI-CAMPFIRES

End your next retreat or camp unusually—with mini-campfires. Have several campfire circles operating simultaneously, and the five to 15 campers in each circle rotate to another circle every 10 or 15 minutes. At each circle a leader could sing a song or two with the group, share a passage of Scripture, give a short talk, and close with prayer. Or each circle's leader could do something creatively different—one plays a biblical person and delivers a modern monologue, another leads worship songs for the full 10 minutes, another simply reads Scriptures, another gets the campers talking about what's happened to them during the weekend.

About the campfires themselves—if you cannot provide actual campfire rings for every group, you can still have a safe fire the following way (as long as you are out of doors; don't use the following method indoors or even under a shelter). Bury a #10 can (the size that most institutional food comes in) three-quarters of the way into the ground. If you cannot put the cans in the ground, pack sand around them so that they're stable. Fill them to within three inches of the top with kerosene (*only* kerosene—no other fuels). Place a rag in the can and light it with a match, and you'll have campfire light for several hours. Smother the kerosene campfires by laying a piece of flat metal on the cans. *Tommy Baker*

CAMP CHARADES

This version of charades is perfect for around-the-campfire fun. Kids must pantomime one of the following actions or things:
• A lightbulb burning out
• A crackling campfire
• One horrendous thunderstorm
• A squeaky bathroom stall door
• A bug crawling on someone's plate
• A snake in the grass
• A rip in someone's pants (you are the rip!)
• A sleeping bag being rolled and unrolled
• Someone being struck by lightning
• Ten mosquitoes biting you all at once
• Gagging on the camp food
• A popcorn kernel thrown into the campfire—it pops and burns up!

Michael A. Nodland

WAR LOG

This is an excellent camp event. Suspend a six-inch pipe (a smooth log could be used) by both ends from tree limbs. Each cabin or team elects a participant. One person gets on each end and tries to knock the other person off with a pillow. No holding onto rope except to get up. Whoever touches the ground, or gets knocked so he or she is hanging upside down three times, loses. Put mattresses underneath for protection. See who can stay on the longest. This is very popular with kids of all ages. *Delbert W. Meliza*

BUCKING BARREL BRONCO

This is a great idea for camps with a Western theme. It does, however, require some work and preparation. Obtain a 55-gallon drum (barrel) and attach (weld, if possible) four eye hooks to it, two on each end. Then attach to each hook heavy ropes or cable that can be tied to four trees or poles, suspending the barrel about four or five feet in the air. A saddle is then fastened to the barrel, and a rider can sit in the saddle. Four big guys then grab the four ropes and pull on them (in an up-and-down manner) as the rider tries to hang on.

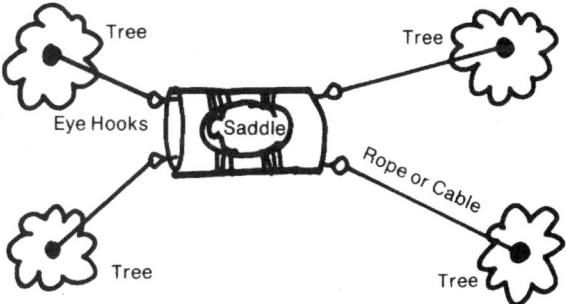

Time riders to see how long they can keep from falling off. It is a good idea to place a mattress under the barrel if the ground is hard. *Roger Disque*

GROUP HUNT

This is a tracking game in which groups try to elude other groups for a period of time in a wooded area, such as at a camp. The groups can be tied together with rope so that they must stick together. The idea is for the groups to move quickly and quietly and to work together as a unit. The game can be made as simple or as complex as you want it to be and may be followed with a discussion relating to cooperation and unity. *Dick Babington*

MUD SLIDE

Why let rain ruin camp? Grass is very slick when it's wet. Pick the steepest convenient and acceptable grassy slope and let the kids slide down with or without plastic toboggans or cardboard. Presently the grass will give out and you'll have a nice mud-slide. *Rogers E. George III*

BOMBS AWAY

Here's a good game for junior high camps. You will need lots of balloons (get the good ones that don't break too easily) and a good wooded area with lots of trees, trails, and so on.

If you have two teams there should only be two different colors of balloons—these are the bombs. If you have more than two teams, then you should have an equal number of balloon colors. Let each

team know what color they are.

Before the game, have your adult counselors hide the balloons. They should be blown up and thumbtacked to trees, logs, etc. They don't have to be hidden very well.

When the campers are released to play the game, they are instructed to try to capture the other team's bombs (unbroken), and to turn them in for points. They also try to find their own team's bombs and destroy them (pop them) before someone from another team can turn them in.

All bombs are turned in for points at a central location where the leader is. Surrounding this area is a Demilitarized Zone, where no one may be attacked. The object is not only to capture the balloons, but to get them safely turned in. Each inflated bomb that is safely turned in is worth 50 points.

If you want to get your thumbtacks back, call them Detonators and give five points for each detonator turned in. That way, even if a bomb is destroyed, a person can still get five points for the detonator. Detonators cannot be taken from a player that already has one in his or her possession. This game is good for about 45 minutes. *Tim Widdowson*

CABIN HIDE 'N' SEEK

Here's an oldie with a new twist. In this version of hide-and-seek, both the hiders and the seekers must do everything by cabin groups, not individually. It's not only fun, but also really helps build the sense of cabin unity that is so important at camp.

The game can be played three times. Each time one-third of the cabins are seekers, while everybody else hides. The seeking cabins can wait somewhere where they can't see (like in an auditorium), and the hiding cabins get 10 minutes to hide. The important rule is that they must hide as a group. In other words, if the cabin decides to hide in a tree, then the whole cabin must get in the tree. If they hide under a building, then the whole cabin must crawl under the building and stay together.

Likewise, the seeking cabins must stick together while they search. The counselors need to reinforce this, or you can give a length of rope to each cabin that everyone must hang onto during the search. Or if you prefer, you could provide a rope (about 20 feet) for all cabins, both those hiding and seeking, and cabin members must be able to touch the rope at all times or they are disqualified.

Set a time limit for the search, and award points as follows: 500 points for staying un-caught and 600 points for catching any cabin. Each round allows a different third of the group to be the seekers. The game is best when played at night, and no flashlights are allowed. After all, it's not easy to hide a whole cabin! *Don Crook*

LOGGERS' FROLIC

By using all natural objects at a campsite or retreat area, you can plan an entire afternoon of games that might have been played at one time by a lumberjack or backwoods logger. It should be set up with a carnival-type atmosphere and it can be used with all ages. You might want to call it Paul Bunyan Day or something like that.

Here are some possible events:

• **Ring Toss.** In the woods there are usually many types of vines. You can fashion them into rings (circles), tied together with twine. Put some stakes in the ground, mark off a throwing line, and award points depending on the difficulty of the toss. If you don't have vines, use rope, wire, or whatever you have.

• **Log Walk.** Cut a log that is about two feet in diameter, and as close to being circular as possible. It is placed at a starting line, and youths try to balance on it and walk it to the finish line. If they fall off, they must start over.

• **Log Rolling.** Use the same log as above. Have two people get on each end and have an old-time contest of trying to roll the other off.

• **Log Pulling.** Cut a log and notch it so that a rope can be tied around it. Kids then compete to pull it a certain distance for the best time. You might have different sizes of logs for different age groups. Or teams can compete pulling on the rope like a tug-o-war.

• **Log Bowling.** Choose a sturdy branch on a tree and tie a rope to it. Then tie on a log, hanging straight down. Stand four slender logs on end around the hanging log. The hanging log then becomes the bowling ball, and it is pulled back about 20 feet, and released to try to knock down the pins.

• **Log Throw.** This is sort of like a javelin throw. Get a long, slender log, and have the kids throw it for distance.
Butch Garman

TRAVOIS RACES

A travois is a primitive vehicle that was used by Native Americans on the plains to move people and cargo. It consists of two trailing poles harnessed to a horse. A platform is then strapped to the back ends of the poles and dragged along the ground. If you don't have a large stable of horses (using them might be dangerous anyway), have travois races using people for the horsepower.

You will need a large pile of slender saplings or small trees eight-to-12-feet long and trimmed of branches. Unless your trees need to be pruned, use

only windfalls rather than stripping branches from live trees. You will also need hammers, nails, and heavy twine. Then map out a lengthy race course, preferably up and down hills and around obstacles.

Divide your group into teams of 12. Each team should choose eight horses and four riders for a four-part relay. The teams should be given 45 minutes to an hour to build their travois. Give assistance as needed.

When everyone is ready, line up the travois on the starting line and send the different relay teams to their respective stops. Each travois should be pulled by two horses and carry one rider seated on the platform. At the first stop, change crews and continue on to the next stop. The true test of durability will be how the travois withstand the race.
Adrienne E. Anderson

SUPERSTAR COMPETITION

Here is an activity that is fun to do anytime but is especially great at camps. The best overall score is the winner. Normally there are 10 events (you may have any number you want). Each participant selects seven to compete in. If you prefer, you can make everyone compete in all of them, but by giving the kids their choice of seven, it helps to equalize things a little bit. In the TV version only the top three contestants in each event score points, but you may want to allow the top 10 in each event to receive points. For example, first place would receive 10 points, second place would get nine points, and so on. If someone were to take first place in all seven of his events (very unlikely), he would get a score of 70 points total.

It is best to choose events that do not give a huge advantage to kids who are athletically inclined, older, smarter, or whatever. This way everyone has a chance and the competition is more fun for everyone involved. Some sample events:
• Water balloon shot put (for distance)
• Shoe kick (hang shoe loosely on foot and kick it for distance)
• Rowboat race (or kayaks or paddling with hands in an inner tube for time)
• Diving (judge for ugliest dive or cannonball, or biggest splash)
• Baseball hitting (use volleyball or have kids hit wrong-handed)
• Sack race (in potato sacks)
• Paper airplane throw (make your own airplane and throw for distance in the air)
• Stilts race (best time)
• Dart throwing (at dartboard or at balloons)
• Math quiz (give kid a problem, must solve it in the fastest time)
• Joke-telling contest or dramatic-reading contest (judged)

At camp certain events can be held each day. Otherwise, you can have all the events going simultaneously, and the kids go from event to event and their scores are recorded in each one that they enter. After everyone is finished winners in each event are declared. Whoever has the most total points is then declared the Superstar and is awarded an appropriate trophy (be creative with this).

Ken Lentz

Your kids need to know—and experience—that not all foreign mission work takes place in foreign countries. So you'll find dozens of ideas for helping overseas missionaries right here at home. A used Bible drive, a bandage-rolling marathon for mission-field hospitals, a scavenger hunt for missionary supplies—these activities not only benefit missionaries, but also help your kids understand the personal, local aspects of mission work.

WRITING A PERSONAL TESTIMONY

Want to ensure that your discipleship group understands the importance of having a prepared testimony as they witness to their friends or during mission or service trips?

This is part Bible study, part written exercise. The Bible study on Paul's conversion is a good opener for your session. Use it inductively as the students read through Acts 26:1-23. Then it's time for your kids to write their own testimonies. Talk through the sections of the worksheet on pages 62-63, allowing kids to verbalize their individual responses to the questions before writing them down. After everyone finishes, ask some—or all—to share their testimonies with each other in small groups. *Vaughn Van Skiver*

USED BIBLE DRIVE

Have you ever counted the number of Bibles you have in your home? Many families have several that are never read. Why not try a Used Bible Drive to put those extra bibles to good use?

Announce to your congregation that you'll be collecting used Bibles and other Christian reading material to be sent to people who have none. Then send the Bibles to World Home Bible League in South Holland, Illinois, which collects used Bibles and distributes them to other countries where they can be used. For more information about the League's program, write or call World Home Bible League, 16801 Van Dam Rd., South Holland, IL 60473; (708) 331-2094; www.biblegue.xc.org/recycle.html *Dawn Cahill*

BANDAGE ROLLING

Bandages are always needed by hospitals overseas in mission fields. By collecting clean old sheets, kids can cut them into strips from two to four inches wide and roll them into bandages for distribution to missionaries and hospitals. One group held a roll-a-thon and secured sponsors who gave 10 cents to one dollar—or as much as they could—per bandage rolled by the youth group in one day. The group wound up with over 600 bandages. *Tom Sykes*

Writing Your Personal Testimony
The Example of the Apostle Paul

One of the privileges and responsibilities of Christians is to share with others our faith in Christ. Although many methods and plans can be used to communicate our faith, none is more effective than sharing how the love, grace, and mercy of Christ has changed our lives.

People to whom we witness may evade issues, attempt to discredit biblical and historical facts, or blame their condition on others. But it's hard to discount the authentic testimony of a believer whose life has been transformed.

That's the reason for this lesson. Completing the worksheet will better equip you to give a logical and organized presentation of who Jesus Christ is and what he has done in your life.

Let's use the story of Paul's conversion in Acts 26:1-23 as a pattern for your testimony.

PAUL'S ATTITUDES AND ACTIONS BEFORE HIS CONVERSION
Read the Bible text: Acts 26:1-23

➥ Lived as a Pharisee—v. 5 (see also Galatians 1:13-14)

➥ Imprisoned many saints—v. 10

➥ Condoned the deaths of many saints—v. 10

➥ Persecuted Christians—v. 11

CIRCUMSTANCES SURROUNDING PAUL'S CONVERSION
Read 2 Corinthians 5:17; Galatians 6:15

1. Where was he going? _____

2. What time was it? _____

3. What did he see? _____

4. Who was with him? _____

5. What did he hear? _____

CHANGES IN PAUL'S ATTITUDES AND ACTIONS AFTER HIS CONVERSION
(Read 1 John 1:5-9; 2:3-6)

What evidence of Paul's repentance and conversion can be found in the following verses:

6. Acts 26:19 _____

7. Acts 26:20 _____

8. Acts 26:21 _____

9. Acts 26:22-23 _____

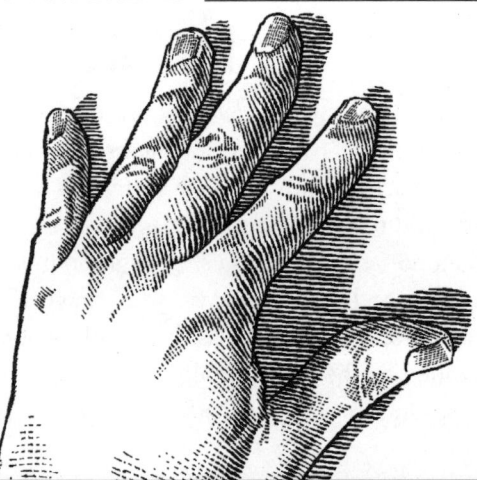

Now go to the next page...

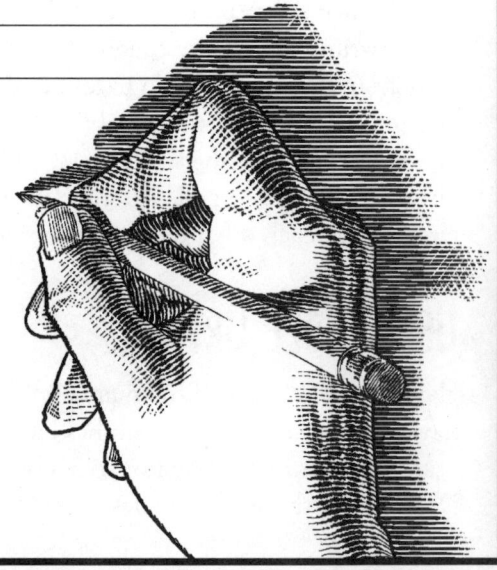

Your Turn!

INTRODUCTION

➡ Name
➡ Year in school (or age)
➡ School
➡ City

ATTITUDES AND ACTIONS BEFORE I BECAME A CHRISTIAN—If appropriate, include family or church background. Avoid naming religious denominations, since this may alienate some of your listeners.

1.

2.

3.

4.

5.

CIRCUMSTANCES SURROUNDING MY CONVERSION—Consider time, date, place, people, motivation, etc.
This is a natural place to summarize the gospel: the death, burial, and resurrection of Jesus Christ.

1.

2.

3.

4.

5.

CHANGES IN MY ATTITUDES AND ACTIONS SINCE MY CONVERSION—Be enthusiastic!

1.

2.

3.

4.

5.

MISCELLANEOUS COMMENTS

M.O.P. TEAMS

M.O.P. stands for Missionary Orientation Program. The idea is to send young people to work with missionaries in the field for a period of time. Teens experience firsthand what the mission field is like. M.O.P. carries a dual meaning because it also shows adults that kids will actually mop floors to make enough money for the trip. Most missionaries are happy to have enthusiastic young people come and help out with various projects for almost any period of time. A program such as this is often the turning point in a young person's life as they attempt to decide just how they want to serve God. *Earl Justice*

MISSIONS SCAVENGER HUNT

Collect items for mission organizations or other charitable groups your church supports by having a Missions Scavenger Hunt. Kids are sent out in teams to go door-to-door asking for specific items from a list of toiletries, household necessities, packaged dry foods, clothes, books, or whatever is needed. Points are awarded for every item collected; the team with the most points wins.

The Missions Scavenger Hunt sheet on page 65 combines this service project with a fun puzzle-solving game. The answers provide the scavenger hunt items. *Sam Crabtree, Craig Carlson, and Kathy Ahlschwede*

BRINGING IN THE SHEAVES

Here's a simple, low-cost way to line up food and provisions for a work camp or service project. Just make up your menu, prepare a shopping list, and post the items needed on a sign-up sheet in your church. Include instructions about when and where to leave donated items. This is a practical approach to stretching a tight service-project budget.

___1 large potato salad	___2 dozen hamburger buns
___1 small jar mustard	___1 large onion
___2 heads lettuce	___2 packages chips
___2 packages chips	___2 gallons milk
___2 gallons milk	___2 loaves wheat bread
___2 loaves white bread	___2 loaves French bread
___4 dozen eggs	___10 pounds oranges
___5 pounds bananas	___2 boxes cold cereal

___2 packages lunchmeats	___2 packages lunchmeats
___1 12-oz package cheese slices	___1 quart jam
___1 12-oz package cheese slices	___2 dozen sweet rolls
___2 large cans vegetable soup	___Hot cocoa mix

Mike Stipe

STAY-AT-HOME WORK CAMP

The idea of a work camp is not new, of course, but many youth groups simply do not have the resources for projects a long way from home. The Stay-at-Home Work Camp combines all the benefits of a work camp without leaving home.

Find a place a few miles out of town where your group can sleep and eat during the whole period of the work camp—four to seven days. The work projects themselves are determined by the needs of your own area and can include painting, remodeling, and construction work on buildings owned by those on fixed incomes such as elderly, widows, or those without income.

Whatever the project, the youths should raise the money for the materials. You could also have members of the church buy scholarships to pay the room and board of each work camper.

To liven up the conference, you can plan activities during the evening for the kids themselves like movies, game nights, etc. Afterward, pictures and a video of the kids working, combined with testimonies from the group, make for quite a program. *Jim Beal*

ADMISSION FOR MISSIONS

To help collect needed supplies for a mission hospital supported by your church or denomination, charge admission to your weekly youth group meetings for a month. Each kid attending must bring one of the following items to get in:

Aspirin (baby and adult)
Multivitamins (with or without iron)
Iron pills
Antibiotic ointments
Adhesive tape
White cotton thread
Sturdy plastic cups and margarine tubs
Containers for the children's ward
Hand soap

...GER HUNT

...s you write!

...r insists that her kids eat their

___ ___ ___ ___ ___.

___, porridge hot,

___, porridge cold,

___, porridge in the pot nine days old.

___ ___, ___ ___ ___ ___ ___, the musical fruit,

...eat the more you toot!

...es are too drab you see,

...ones of color to me!

...packaging, it comes on something that rhymes

...___ ___ ___ on the ___ ___ ___.

...ouldn't give these up for anything. What's Up

___ ___ ___ ___

...nock.

...ere?

...who?

...nock.

...ere?

...who?

...nock.

...ere?

...who?

Orange you glad I didn't say banana!

7. A game is played where you sit in a circle and pass an object that is hot. What is it? A ___ ___ ___ ___ ___ ___.

8. Every relish dish has this. Is not red, but it is green. If you eat enough, you'll stay LEAN: ___ ___ ___ ___ ___ ___.

9. You will see a smile on their faces when you ask for a pair of red shoelaces.

10. What do Chun King, Elizabeth Taylor, and Uncle Ben all have in common? ___ ___ ___ ___.

17. Collect four types of #16.

18. A green zipper (for no good reason).

19. This will take the gum out of your hair if you dare to dab it there: ___ ___ ___ ___ ___ ___ ___ ___ ___ ___

Instant soup
Baby cereal
Scrub brushes
Sanitary napkins
Twill tape
Hand towels
Razor blades (old-fashioned type)
Sheet blankets
Nursing uniforms (specify colors, sizes, and fabric types)
Men's uniform tops

Adjust the list to fit your own mission hospital's needs. *Tommy Martin*

SUPPLY SCAVENGER HUNT

If your group is planning a mission trip that requires donated supplies—tools, building materials, clothing, etc.—consider having a Supply Scavenger Hunt a few weeks before the trip. Send your young people into the community with a list similar to the one below, and you will be amazed at how many good, usable items your kids will bring back. It's a worthwhile activity—and fun, too!

Hammer (part or whole)
Rake (broken or whole—we can heal broken handles)
Work gloves (any condition)
Concrete-working gloves (rubber)
Pick (of any sort)
Plastic safety goggles
Brownies or chocolate-chip cookies
Hoe (any condition)
One box of framing nails
Old concrete trowel (any style)
Wheelbarrow (dare you to find someone who gives this to you!)
Shovel (extra points if it's in good condition)

Steve Mabry

MISSION TO MISSION

Want to get your kids thinking about world missions? Want them to feel connected to real-life missionaries? Arrange a speaker-phone call from your youth group to an overseas missionary. It's easy to do, encourages the missionary, and opens teenagers' eyes to real life on the mission field.

Get the address and phone number of an over-seas missionary that your church supports; a missionary family with a teenage son or daughter is best. Call or write them to determine their interest in and availability for talking to your group. Arrange a date and time, and prep them with questions students might ask.

When a missionary is scheduled and prepped, then calendar a Missions Activity Night that highlights the missionary you'll call. Often you can keep the Q&A session organized by selecting a student to be the spokesperson during the call.

After the call discuss with your group the mechanics of becoming a missionary, what it requires, etc., or the process of actively supporting the work of a missionary through letters, prayer, and financial support. If the time is right, suggest that the group consider keeping in touch with the missionary on a regular basis through telephone calls, e-mail, and care packages. When the missionary comes stateside on furlough, arrange a face-to-face reunion between the missionary and your group. *Cheryl Ehlers*

MIX WITH MISSIONARIES NIGHT

Here is a creative way to help your teens interact with and learn from visiting missionaries. Invite several missionaries and their families to this event. Play some of the following games and then serve refreshments while teens and missionaries mingle freely.

• **Missionary Jeopardy!** Play it the same way as the TV game show "Jeopardy!" but make all questions pertain to particular mission fields or common misconceptions about missionaries. Have the missionaries help you prepare the questions and answers ahead of time.

• **Missionary Bingo.** Fill squares with descriptions about your missionaries (see page 67 for an example). Consult with your missionaries for specific questions and answers as needed. Have teens get the appropriate missionaries to initial the boxes. Teens can put their own initials in the box in the center of their cards. Award a prize to the first teen who acquires initials in a complete row horizontally, vertically, or diagonally. You can also award a prize to the teen who gets all squares initialed first. Before the game begins, tell teens that the winners will present their prizes to the missionary of their choice. Make the prizes something a missionary could use—Christian books, magazines, T-shirts, etc.

• **Missionary Mad Lib.** Ask your group to supply you with a noun, an adjective, a boy in your group, and the rest of the categories identified under the blanks on page 68. Then read the mad lib using the supplied words.

You can end with a question and answer session. Intersperse questions like these with questions your teens ask:

• What made you think God wanted you to become a missionary?

• What is it like to live in a foreign country?

• Why did you go so far away when there are spiritual needs here?

A session like this can create interest in and a sense of responsibility for missionaries from your church. *Rich Starcher*

Missionary Bingo

I'm a teaching missionary	I speak Spanish	I am currently translating the New Testament	I have three children	I was a pastor before I became a missionary
My mission field is the Philippines	I'm a church-planting missionary	I'm not from Nebraska	My mission field is Japan	I speak Japanese
I've eaten raw fish	I speak only English	You	I'm a missionary's kid	I play the flute
I graduated from Trinity College	I've been a missionary for more than 15 years	My mission field is Mexico	I've been a missionary for less than one term	I used to serve in Africa
I'm originally from Wisconsin	I became a missionary after attending a conference in Urbana	I like sports	I'm a missionary on an Indian reservation	I like to cook native dishes

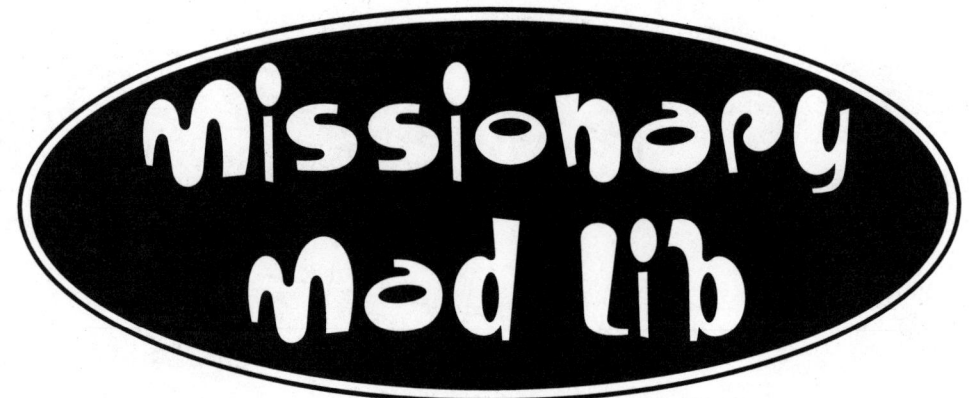

Once upon a _____ there was a _____ young man named
(noun)   (adjective)

_____. One _____ _____ _____ decided that the Lord
(boy in group)   (adjective)   (day)   (same boy)

wanted him to be a missionary to _____. The only problem was
                                  (name of place)

_____ was _____ in love with _____, and he knew she
(same boy)   (adverb)   (girl in group)

would never _____ to live in a _____ place like _____.
                (verb)   (adjective)   (same place)

What was _____ to do?
          (same boy's name)

After _____ thought, he decided to _____ it straight.
       (adjective)   (verb)

_____, he said, you know I _____ you _____, but the Lord
(same girl)   (verb)   (adverb)

has told me to go to _____ as a _____. Will you go with me as
                      (same place)   (noun)

my _____? _____, she exclaimed, I'd _____ to _____
   (noun)   (exclamation)   (verb)   (verb)

in _____. They eat _____ _____, and _____
   (same place)   (adjective)   (plural noun)   (plural noun)

and _____ _____ there, and those are my favorites. Of
    (adjective)   (plural noun)

course, I'll _____ with you.
              (verb)

And so they lived _____ ever after.
                   (adverb)

Teenagers, like most of us, tend to be self-centered by nature. So a valuable service you can do for your kids is to expose them to the needs of others. Enter the following pages of ideas—where you'll find suggestions for helping children, the community at large, the elderly, the poor and homeless, shut-ins, and the sick and disabled. You may be surprised at how readily your group members respond when they are confronted by people in need.

SENSITIZING ACTIVITIES

TEN STEPS TO ACTION

Seeing problems in the world is easy, but doing something about them usually isn't. To help kids see what they can do, give the following instructions one at a time, allowing enough time for kids to think through each point. Discussion can follow.

1. List five social problems in your community.
2. Circle three that the church can tackle.
3. Underline two of those you can do.
4. Rewrite one of these two.
5. List five things to be done to deal with this problem.
6. Circle two you can do.
7. Underline one you will do.
8. What will hinder you from accomplishing the task?
9. What will help you to do it?
10. Will you do it?

Homer Erekson

CHURCH WHO'S WHO

Looking for a way to increase the sensitivity of your kids to the rest of your church body? Consider a church-family information book. Using the church

membership roll, assign the name of every individual and family in the church to a group of two or three youths who will make an appointment to visit them. Send with the youths a list of questions resembling those on a census: number of family members, ages, birth dates, place of birth, employment, school attending (or attended), degrees obtained, hobbies, interests.

The information the groups obtains can be stored on computer and updated annually. Students can also compile a booklet to distribute during a second visit to each family, thus insuring that each church family is visited twice a year. The youths become involved in visiting others—especially those that they don't know, relationships develop between the generations, and church members gain a valuable resource. *Greg Miller*

CHILDREN

NURSERY RENOVATION

It's difficult to find a service project that all members of a youth group will tackle with enthusiasm, but you may strike oil with this one. Most of the kids in your group probably baby-sit, and many of them may help keep the church nursery at various times during the week. If so, they would probably be eager to do something for the little tykes (and their parents). If the church nursery leaves a few things to be desired, why not let the teens renovate it?

Devote a work day or lock-in to clean the windows, paint the rocking chairs, scrub and repair the mattresses, clean and disinfect the toys, wash the walls and woodwork, make colorful cushions and matching curtain valances, and shampoo the carpet. If the walls are drab, paint them or put up bright posters.

The congregation will be convinced that the youth really care about the church and the little kids. And the teenagers will be proud that they've done something that's tangible and practical.

Robin Garrett

SUMMER JAMBOREE

This is a creative alternative to Vacation Bible School. The youths of the church put on a Summer Jamboree for children in a low-rent housing area. Find a building in the area for the activities, crafts, Bible stories, films, hikes, picnics,

games, etc. Run it for a week, advertise it, and watch kids flock to it since it has been brought to them in their neighborhood. Invite the families of the children one day to see the activities and a program put on by the kids. This idea has been very successful, and more effective than the usual VBS, which tends to be overly churchy. *Leroy Albertson*

THROW A PARTY FOR THE LITTLE KIDS

Enlist the senior high youths to put on a party for kids in Sunday school grades one through six. This gives the senior high kids a service project and is great fun for the younger kids. When the guests arrive, divide them into two groups—grades one through three and four through six. Let one group go through a carnival set up in the Sunday school classrooms. The other group would have active games. After about 45 minutes, switch the two groups. Then show a Christian film geared to children and serve refreshments. *William C. Moore*

BABY-SITTING CO-OP

If your church Sunday School facilities are vacant during the summer, look into the possibility of a baby-sitting co-op for service or for fundraising. Arrange to have baby-sitting available for a few hours each day by appointment, and sign up members of the youth group to sit one day a week or less depending on the size of the group. You'll be surprised at how many grateful mothers will leave their youngsters for baby-sitting while they go shopping or to meetings or to the pool. However, you must be careful about which ages you'll be able to accept and that there will always be enough teens or adults on hand for good child supervision. *Ellen Sutter*

TOY COLLECTION

Every town has some organization that collects toys at Christmas for needy children. A good group activity would be to have a toy drive in the fall. The kids go door-to-door to collect old unwanted toys that are still usable or that require minor repairs. The kids can clean up and repair the toys, if necessary, and then distribute them or give them to an agency that distributes them. This can be made into a contest for teams to see who can collect and salvage the most toys within a given time limit. *Jim Berkeley*

PARENTS' NIGHT OUT

Use this idea to give adults in your church a night out, provide a service project for your youth, plus make a little money for your next retreat or trip fund.

Offer adults a night out that provides a simple dinner, an entertaining movie, and babysitting services all for one low price.

Set up TVs and VCRs, and chairs as needed. Have the group prepare and set up for the dinner (along with beverages and store-bought dinner rolls, you can serve soup or quiche and salad, chili, or the like, and ice cream for dessert); then divide the team in half. One half serves the adults, while the other half feeds and cares for the kids in another room. Then they switch. Half the group cleans up, while the other half baby-sits. Afterward, all the youth work together to tidy up. If there's time, kids may want to stay later to see the movie for themselves. *Rodney Puryear*

THE COMMUNITY

TALENTS IN ACTION

For one intense day, teenagers can work with and learn from a skilled adult—and then use that newly acquired skill in serving others.

The first part of the day looks like a talent fair. Adults in your congregation that are skilled in virtually any field—large- and small-engine repair, sports, cooking, baby-sitting, reupholstery, home maintenance, photography, drama, sewing, etc.—use the morning to teach their own small group of kids a simple but practical skill, such as car engine tune-up and lube. That afternoon the kids tune up and lube vehicles that belong to your church's older members. Or having made prearranged plans with a local hospital or convalescent home, the

drama instructor takes his team there to perform in the afternoon.

A one-day workshop like this takes a lot of planning. However, it pays off not only in the immediate application of what's learned, but also in the intergenerational contact between adults and teenagers. *Wib Newton*

ECO-MUG A HOUSE

The sample flier on page 74 says it all. *Kent Busman*

P.E.T.S.

Form a P.E.T.S. team (**P**eople **E**ncouraging **T**hrough **S**ervice) of young people to serve specially targeted groups in the church. Meet one night a week to perform services according to these priorities:
• **Hospital Calls.** Make and deliver poster-size get well cards for church members and acquaintances in the hospital. Spend 10 minutes or so with the patient, putting the poster on the wall, chatting, and praying together. If you can, give a bouquet of balloons as well.
• **Absentee Calls.** If no one's in the hospital, check the youth group attendance records for names of kids who have been absent four straight weeks or more. Make posters covered with faces and the message, "We Miss Your Face!" Then take it to their homes. They usually come the next week!
• **Birthday and Anniversary Calls.** If no one's in the hospital or on the critically absent list, check the church rolls for birthday and wedding anniversaries. Make and deliver cards accordingly.
• **Encouragement Calls.** When no one's in any of these categories on a particular night, make posters for anyone who could use an uplift. Pay them a short visit.

This program scatters around lots of joy, gives the kids a sense of ministry, and provides great PR for the youth program. *Randy Wheeler*

TRUCK TROOPS

To help people with those project-sized chores that require a pickup truck, schedule your group's teenage truck owners for Truck Troop missions.

Get your house

Eco-Mugged

The Senior Youth Group, in keeping with its environmental concern, wants to help you help us . . .

Save the Earth

HOW? By letting us **Eco-Mug** your house.
We will come in at a predetermined time and . . .

- Get your name off junk-mail lists
- Install a toilet dam
- Check the air in your tires for proper inflation
- Install one faucet aerator
- Leave a handmade Youth Group Draft Dodger to keep cold air from getting in under your door
- Leave a hand-painted Youth Group Eco-Mug
- Leave you with three beautiful note cards printed on recycled paper
- Take your unwanted clothing to an appropriate donation center

What better gift to give to a friend and our world!

Cost for getting Eco-Mugged is $30
All proceeds will go to our Youth Group Spring Break "Give 'Em a Break"

We estimate that if 100 families get **Eco-Mugged** we could each year . . .

SAVE
150 trees to sit in the shade under
622,000 gallons of fresh water to swim in or enjoy
3,000 gallons of gas to enjoy cleaner air with
36,500 disposable cups

HAVE
100 more comfortable houses to wait out winter's cold in
300 more people told about saving God's earth through letters written on recycled paper
100 more people living with better clothes and dignity

- Based on research done in *50 Simple Things You Can Do to Save the Earth*

☐**YES!** I want my house Eco-Mugged.
Here is my $30 gift to help save the earth.

Name _____

Address _____

City _____ State _____

Zip _____

Phone (home) _____

(work) _____

Divide the youth group into Truck Troop teams that can haul and stack firewood, move furniture to storage, make a run to the city dump, deliver used furniture or appliances to the needy, etc. Advertise the service in your newsletter or church bulletin. You'll have plenty of takers and some unusual opportunities for ministry within your congregation and community. *Bert Jones*

PARTY-MAKING PARTY

This is a great idea for youth groups that are tired of having parties and tired of helping others. Have your youth group put on a party for those groups you want to help. You could organize a Sweetheart's Banquet for an old folks home or the elderly in your congregation; an Easter Egg Hunt for an orphanage or special education group; a Christmas party for underprivileged kids; or a Thanksgiving Banquet for underprivileged kids, widows, or college students away from home. *Stephen Douglas Williford*

RAKE AND SHAKE

This fall combine a service day of raking leaves in the yards of church members with fun and games. Allow about 45 minutes per home if 10 kids rake. Publicize ahead of time that games like these will be played in yards along the way: candy-bar hunt,

leaf football (the football is a bag of leaves), pile-on, leaf-bag fight (like a pillow fight), leaf relays, leaf hockey (rakes are sticks), and any other rowdy leaf games they can concoct along the way.

Leave a thank-you card at each home, and wind up back at the church for hot chocolate.

• Rake and Run

Load up all the kids in a bus and arm each with a lawn rake. Go up and down streets and whenever you see a lawn that needs raking, everyone jumps out and rakes all the leaves up. No pay is accepted for any of the work. It is all done in the name of Christ. You might find out the names of shut-ins who cannot rake their own lawns as specific homes

Be sure to join us in our "Rake & Run" Party this Saturday afternoon from 1:00 until 4:00.

Bring a leaf rake (If you have one) Wear old clothes. We'll ride the bus to various deserving homes and rake their leaves and then run to the next one.

We'll eat too!

Lots of fun while we do something worthwhile for others.

to visit. This activity can be both fun and rewarding for the kids. During the winter, kids can shovel snow in the same way. You can call it Snow and Blow. *Glenn Zimbelman and Arthur Merkle*

SPLASH AND SPLIT

The youth group travels up and down streets washing windows on houses. Of course, the people who live in the house should be asked first, but usually it's rare for anyone to turn it down. The group should do it for free, just as a way to show the community that Christian love is more than just words.

This can also be done to raise money for a mission or service project if donations are accepted for the window washing. Take whatever people feel that they can pay, or charge a modest fee, like $5 per house. With a group of five or 10 kids, the job can be done rather quickly with everyone taking two or three windows. *Scott Dell*

SERVANT SEARCH

Here's a service project that will challenge your kids to creative servanthood. Divide your large group into small groups of two or three. Tell them they have exactly one hour to penetrate the community and serve it in some fashion. The goal is to serve as many people as possible in any way possible. Be creative: Some students will sweep the sidewalks, others will go door-to-door asking to wash windows or pull weeds, and others will pick up trash in a local parking lot or field. Some may even go to a local gas station and pump gas for people at the self-serve islands. No one is allowed to receive money for the services.

At the end of the hour, the students return to tell about their experience. Award prizes for the most creative, hardest workers, most people served, and so on. Give lots of affirmation to each team. It will help build self-esteem in your students and encourage them to be self-starters. *Alan Hamilton*

FREE LOVE

In a very simple but effective sharing ministry, kids go door-to-door in a local neighborhood and ask if there is anything they can do—for free. People are stunned that a stranger is actually volunteering to do their dishes, vacuum carpets, wash their car, mow their lawn, etc. They usually want to know what the gimmick is, but the kids reply, "We're just trying to show our love for God by passing that love on to others." One group made the front page of the *Chicago Tribune* with this service project.

A variation of this is to take the youth group into a shopping center and do the same thing. Carry packages for people, wash car windows, etc. A message can be left under the windshield wipers: "Your window was washed by a Christian just trying to say 'God loves you.'" A revolutionary approach to witnessing. *Lee Eclor*

SATURDAY SERVANTS

To give your youth a regular chance to serve church members with special needs, designate occasional Saturday mornings (9:00 a.m. to noon) as the time for Saturday Servants. Use a bulletin insert announcing the project two weeks in advance so that church members who need assistance can call the church ahead of time with their requests.

Saturday Servants focus primarily—though not necessarily exclusively—on performing chores for the elderly, shut-ins, widows, divorced persons, and single parents in the church. Jobs to be done might be anything from yard work to child care, car maintenance to furniture moving. It's a good idea to ask the people being served to provide the necessary equipment and cleaning supplies if possible.

Your youths will find that their sacrifice of time and energy on a Saturday morning can provide a significant and practical ministry to many members of the church. *Gary Wrisberg*

WINDSHIELD WITNESSING

Find a parking lot with a lot of cars in it and supply the youth group with window cleaning materials (soap, rags, squeegees, etc.). The kids move up and down rows in twos and clean dirty windshields on cars, leaving a note similar to this:

> Your windows have been cleaned with love by the youth of Main St. Community Church. We just wanted to do something nice for people today to demonstrate the love of Christ, and we hope that's okay with you. We also hope you'll see your way clear to attend the church of your choice next Sunday!

Some people may want to make a donation to the youth group, but make sure the kids do this strictly for free. People will really appreciate it. *Alan R. Vranian*

A CUP OF COOL WATER IN HIS NAME

This is both a service project and an opportunity to witness for Christ! Youths from any church near beaches or other recreational areas where large groups of people gather can do this. Materials needed are a five-gallon cooler filled with ice water and paper cups. The cooler can be pulled in a wagon or may be carried by a guy on a backpack frame. The water is usually appreciated by people on a hot summer day, when offered at no charge, with a smile and perhaps a word about "Living Water" (John 4). It can be a positive way to share Christ with people. *Mike Weaver*

ECOLOGICAL SCAVENGER HUNT

The following is a good activity for get-togethers at the beach or a picnic and park area. Give the kids a list of the following items that must be found on the ground. No taking from garbage cans allowed! Give points for each item found. Set no limit per item so that someone can bring back 25 aluminum cans and collect 25 points). Also, award bonus points for the most different items on the list; for example, if anyone brings in at least one of every item on the list, he might get a bonus of 100 points. If he brings back seven different items, 75 bonus points could be awarded, etc. Here is a sample list:

Candy wrapper	Aluminum beverage can
Plastic fork	Paper cup
Plastic spoon	Gum wrapper
Paper plate	Pop or beer bottle
Napkin	Article of clothing

All items must be brought in complete. No tearing things in half and counting them twice. You may add items to the list as you see fit, depending on where you do it. Give everyone a plastic trash bag to collect stuff in, and provide a prize for the winner. *Phil Miglioratti*

ECOLOGY WALK

This walk incorporates two ideas and can be very successful with a group of 25 or more. First of all, as in a regular walkathon, kids get sponsors. Then, as the kids walk, they pick up all the aluminum cans that litter the highways. Have someone follow along and pick up full containers in a truck. Divide the kids in groups of five or six and send them each in a different direction with plastic bags that they can leave filled at the side of the road. If you have

a good day, you can easily pick up between 500 and 1,000 pounds of aluminum to be recycled. *Daniel Unrath*

FREE CAR WASH

Set up a youth car wash at a local shopping center or filling station as you normally would. However, instead of charging for the wash tickets, give them away. Advertise it as a free car wash. Make it clear that there are no strings attached. People may get their car washed free by the youth of your church simply because it is a gesture of Christian love and friendship.

However, those who care to may make a contribution of any amount they choose. This money can then be used by the youth for a missionary project, a relief agency providing food for famine stricken countries, or other worthy projects.

A sign may be posted at the car wash site similar to this one:

> **Your car is being washed by the youth of _____ church for free with no strings attached. It's just one small way for us to demonstrate to you the love of Jesus Christ. Another way we are attempting to share Christ's love is by collecting funds to help purchase food for the hungry. If you would like to help us with this project, your contribution would be greatly appreciated. Thank you and God bless you.**

Of course, your version of this sign would depend on what you were raising money for, but avoid using this to simply increase the coffers of the church building fund or the youth group's social activities fund. You can print this information on the tickets as well, and many people will come prepared to give.

One youth group did this twice and raised a total of $800, strictly through contributions received at their free car washes. Pick a busy location, make sure you have plenty of hardworking, friendly kids, and the experience can be very rewarding. *Gary Close*

GIFT OF LOVE

An effective way for young people to exercise their faith is through helping others without regard to getting anything in return. Try mailing a letter such as the one below to homes in your community and see what develops. *Alyce Redwine*

Dear friend,

The members of the church Youth Fellowship want to show appreciation for our special friends by a work day. Can we help you in some way? Does your lawn need mowing? Do you need help getting groceries? Would you want windows washed? Would you like us to read to you? Just visit you?

Just mark on the enclosed card how we can be of some help. If we receive a reply from you, we will come on _____. Please indicate whether you prefer morning or afternoon.

Of course, there is no charge. This is a gift of love.

PORTABLE MCDONALD'S

If your church or organization is located in or near a college community, here's a great way to get involved with college students. During registration or the first week of class, plan a hamburger snack for the students. Advertise by passing out flyers and posters throughout the campus. Locate the snack bar on or near campus and have plenty of people from your group to serve and mingle with the kids when they come. The food is provided by asking each family in the church to bring something like a package of buns, hamburger, potato chips, etc.

Rick Trexler

PROJECT DOORKNOB

Distribute flyers around the community announcing that next Saturday (or whenever) your youth group will be passing by in the church bus looking for work to do. If anyone would like some help, simply tie a handkerchief onto the doorknob of your front door. As a service project, this work can be offered free to the community. As a fundraiser, you might ask for a 50-cent donation (per hour) or something like that. You'll be amazed at how many people will take advantage of this offer. *Don Snider*

SERVANT WEEK

Here is a summer activity that not only can involve all of your youth group, but is a real witness and ministry to the community. Your particular schedule of events would vary, or course, depending on the needs of your community, but the sample schedule below should stimulate your creative thinking.

- **Sunday.** Young people take part in regular church with a presentation to their own community of believers and follow with coffee or refreshments.
- **Monday.** The youth group provides free coffee and doughnuts for commuters at train or subway location. If there are any left over, distribute them to local police stations, fire stations, city offices, or businesses.
- **Tuesday.** Senior Citizens Day. Have your youth group visit local nursing homes and provide programs such as talent shows, puppet shows, etc. Have the kids talk and play games with the elderly in these homes. Sponsor an ice cream party for the elderly of the church and the community in the evening.
- **Wednesday.** Children's Day. Plan activities for kids, such as puppet shows in the city park and at children's wards in hospitals. Offer free baby-sitting for parents to go out by themselves.
- **Thursday.** City Government Day. Kids can spend more time providing help and services to the city. End the day with an Appreciation Banquet put on entirely by the kids for the city leaders and business people.
- **Friday.** The entire youth group offers its services to the city to provide help in an area of need (the

group that submitted this idea helped the city cut a trail in the city's open space—very difficult and back-breaking work). This activity needs to be negotiated with proper officials in advance.

The above ideas are only suggestions, of course. Your group should find things to do every day that meet needs, demonstrate Christian love and concern, and are realistic (within the ability of the group to accomplish). The group that contributed this idea had a number of flyers printed which said in essence: "Hi, we're the youth group from (name of church) and we just want to let you know that we want to serve you if you will let us. We don't want to sell you anything, solicit a donation, or try to get new church members. We are just trying to learn to obey the Lord by serving." "Through love, serve one another." (Gal. 5:13)

If you spend time preparing well for Servant Week, you'll find that not only will your youth group learn a lot, but they will grow closer together, and the community will benefit from many acts of kindness. *Ridge Burns*

THE ELDERLY

WINTERIZE YOUR ELDERLY

Raking leaves is only the beginning of what needs to be done for the shut-ins and the elderly of your church, especially if you live in the northern latitudes. Before cold weather sets in, your teens can put up storm windows, change furnace filters, haul in patio furniture, take down porch awnings—a difficult or impossible chore for the elderly, but the work of an hour or two for energetic young people.

And don't forget them the following spring when the houses must be returned to warm-weather condition and the lawns mowed. *Howard Chapman*

WIDOW AND WIDOWER DINNER

To get your kids together with the older folks in your church, have the youth group plan, prepare, and serve—at tables, not buffet style—a dinner for the widows and widowers. After the meal provide entertainment: old movies, group singing, games. Whoever isn't part of the entertainment can take care of cleanup. The people served will be so grateful and the kids will have so much fun, that it just might become an annual event! *Dawn Cahill*

SMOKE ALARM MINISTRY

This service project could literally save lives. Have your youths install battery-operated smoke detectors in the homes of the elderly of your community.

First, decide how detectors and batteries will be purchased or donated. Around Christmas many department stores will sell minimum quantities at wholesale. Better yet, the local fire marshal's office usually has connections to suppliers who will donate the detectors if the group doing the installations will make a list of persons serviced.

Second, prepare a list of elderly people who might need the service. Then perform a phone survey asking if these people would welcome teens into their homes to install the smoke detector for free. Youths could also check the batteries for smoke detectors already in place. Arrange a time—usually an entire Sunday afternoon—when the senior citizens would be home to receive the service team.

Third, find out if the fire marshal can also provide slides, films, or volunteer speakers who will come in a week before the project to sensitize youths to general fire safety practices, as well as to the specific risks facing the elderly. Because a disproportionate number of fires occur in the homes of older people, this project could mean the difference between life and death. *Mark Forrester*

YOUNG AND WISE BANQUET

This event is both a service project and a fun activity for youth groups. The young people plan a banquet, complete with a banquet program, and invite the senior citizens of the church to come as their guests. The youths either pay for the food to be catered, bring it potluck-style, or prepare it themselves. However, it is usually best that the kids not have to spend too much time with meal preparation, as they need time to spend with their guests.

Each kid is assigned certain senior citizens to

pick up, take home, and sit with during the banquet. Invitations are sent to the senior citizens along with RSVP forms that they can send back. Be sure to plan a menu that senior citizens can eat and keep the program brief and lively. To be sure of a successful evening, make plans quite a few weeks in advance and promote it well. One church has done this two years in a row with more than 175 senior citizens attending each year. *Larry Osborne*

DESSERT DESERT

Dessert Desert is a fun service project for your group. Have the kids line up several pies, cakes, and other desserts to be donated by people in the

Dear: _____
You have just become a victim of **"Dessert Desert."** The youth group from the Church of the Nazarene thought you might enjoy a delectably delicious pie made by some of our very own people in the church.
Enjoy and God Bless!

church. Then let them deliver the desserts to the doorsteps of elderly people or shut-ins by ringing the doorbell and running. The recipient opens the door to find a pie and a little note as shown in the illustration. Try one on the steps of the police department! *Jim Halbert*

ADOPT A GRANDPARENT

Here is a great service project that can be done close to home. It is best for more mature young people who are willing to make a long-term commitment to something.

After visiting a convalescent home or other homes of elderly people who are basically alone, introduce the idea to the group. Ask the young people if they would be willing to adopt one or more of these elderly people as a grandparent. This would involve visiting them on a regular basis, remembering them on special occasions, taking them places when necessary, and just being a good friend over a long period of time—as long as possible. This project should include times that the young people share with each other how things are going and what problems they are encountering.

Most young people will find this to be an

extremely rewarding experience, and the elderly people will appreciate it greatly. *William C. Moore*

OVER 65 PARTY

The youth of the church throw a party for the senior citizens of the community. Play games, serve refreshments, sing old-time songs, and do things *with* them, rather than just having them watch. It makes the old folks feel a little younger, helps the kids learn to appreciate the elderly, and makes a great service project. *Dawn Boyd*

SACRIFICIAL MEAL

After church some Sunday serve the youth group a sacrificial meal consisting of rice and tea (Asian diet) or beans and tortillas (Chicano diet). Charge each person for the meal and give all the money to a group like World Vision. Use videos, literature, Bible passages, music tapes, poems, and spoken experiences from someone who has seen the results of hunger. *Don Mason*

H.O.P. CLUB

H.O.P. stands for **H**elp **O**lder **P**eople and the H.O.P. Club is a program for teens and adults to work together in assisting the elderly with work they are unable to do for themselves. This should be an ongoing ministry as opposed to a one-shot service project. Skilled adults train the youth to do carpentry, plumbing, wiring, upholstery, or whatever needs to be done, and give direction and supervision while on the job. Younger kids can be involved in such tasks as washing windows and walls, raking leaves, shoveling snow, moving furniture, writing letters, and so on. Many other people who want to be involved, but less directly, can provide financial assistance, rides etc. The important thing is that it should be well-organized, and carried out on a regular basis. Many senior citizen's groups can provide information on where the greatest needs are and inform the elderly community that this service is available at no charge or at a very low cost.

A program such as this not only provides valuable relief for the elderly, who must pay to have this work done, but also gives kids the opportunity to give of themselves in a meaningful way and to build relationships with a segment of society they often ignore. *Terry Stoops*

BREAD-BAKING BASH

Have the kids in your youth group gather up all the ingredients they need to bake up lots of bread—both loaves and rolls. Then organize a Saturday of bread baking, first preparing the dough, getting it into pans, and then letting it rise. While it's doing that, the kids can play games and socialize until the bread is baked.

When the bread is finished, prepare some soup and have a lunch featuring hot soup and freshly baked bread. You might have everyone bring a can of soup—any kind—and mix it all together. After lunch, wrap the remaining loaves and visit the homes of some elderly people in the church. Spend a short time visiting with them and leave them with a loaf of homemade bread and a note of appreciation, like "Thanks for being a part of our church family." They'll love it, and it really helps to build relationships between the young and the old. You could conclude the day with a discussion of what happened while visiting the elderly and perhaps a Bible lesson relating to bread. *Jim Elder*

THE POOR AND HOMELESS

SOCK GIVEAWAY

This year don't bless the socks off the needy in your community. For a change, bless the needy *with* socks!

Decorate shoe boxes with a sock motif and place them throughout the church. By means of signs and fliers, ask those who attend church or Sunday school to donate money for the youth group to purchase socks for needy children through an approved community agency. After three weeks, the group goes shopping for socks with the money collected.

The following week decorate the meeting room

with socks—old socks, new socks, Christmas socks, huge socks, teeny socks—and display in some way the socks the group purchased to give away. Celebrate the collection effort with a sock hop—everyone must wear socks they decorated at home. Offer crazy prizes for the prettiest, ugliest, scariest, and funniest socks. Then turn up some oldies and dance the limbo, the twist, and the pony.

The day after the sock hop, take the new socks to the agency. *Mary Jo Mastin*

BINGO SCAVENGER HUNT

Divide youths into carloads. Use the bingo card like the one on page 82—it names foods to be collected within a certain time limit. Add your own specific instructions, time limits, etc. You may allow them to collect items door-to-door in a particular neighborhood, or limit them to only their own or other church members' homes. They can collect only one item per house visited.

The object is to collect items from the same row or diagonal to get a bingo. The first team back with a bingo wins. The collected items are donated to the needy. *Cheryl Ehlers*

SANDWICHES FOR THE HOMELESS

Canned and bulk food are appropriate for the poor who have kitchens and ranges and ovens—but street people don't have even these. Peanut butter and jelly sandwiches, on the other hand, are inexpensive, easy to prepare and keep (they freeze well), universally liked, and fairly high in nutritional value.

With the guidance of your community food closet, spend a day with your group in your church kitchen or at the food closet making peanut butter and jelly sandwiches for the homeless. Solicit food from bakeries and markets, and let your congregation give cash gifts in order to purchase the food and supplies that aren't donated. Or ask all members of your group to bring either a jar of peanut butter or jelly—depending on the first letter of their last name. Organization for a party like this is crucial—delegate workers to provide counter space, knives, cleanup, delivery to the food closet, and thank-you notes to those who made donations. *Larry Emery*

Bingo
Scavenger Hunt

can of green beans	box of Jell-O	box of crackers	can of evaporated milk	bottle of shampoo
box of light bulbs	can of soup	box of hot cereal	bar of soap	box of salt
can of refried beans	jar of jelly	can of hot chocolate mix	box of cereal	package of spaghetti noodles
jar of peanut butter	cake mix	jar of applesauce	bag of sugar	box of raisins
can of fruit	box of rice	roll of toilet paper	jar of spaghetti sauce	tube of toothpaste

SOUP KITCHEN SUPPORT

If your church wants to help feed the hungry, but you're in an area where there would not be enough needy people to warrant a soup kitchen, try this idea. Set up a market table in the fellowship hall or a Sunday school room for church members to bring produce from their own gardens for others to buy. Items can be purchased for a freewill donation rather than a set price.

The money raised from this project can then be sent to help support a soup kitchen in another area. Though the market table involves only a minimum of preparation and organization, it can generate a useful sum for ministry to the hungry. *Frank Billman*

CLOTHES SEARCH

This service project idea can be done with individuals or in small groups. Give the kids a list of clothes needed by an organization you are familiar with. Contact this group ahead of time to find out what items they need most and adjust points accordingly. The kids or groups then have two hours to accumulate as many points as possible. They must start at their own house and go from there. Here is a typical list:

Pants and jeans—25 points for pants, 50 points for jeans
Dresses—70 points per dress
Coats—150 points for small sizes, 100 points for large sizes
Shirts—20 points
Sweaters—40 points
Underwear—50 points for washed, 5 points for unwashed
Cloth diapers—200 points
Shoes—175 points
Pajamas—15 points
Infant clothing—250 points

You can also set up bonus houses. These are homes where the people have collected some clothes already. Each person or group is given a clue sheet. The first person or group to decipher the clues and get to the bonus house gets the clothes at that home.

The group that originally did this activity stipulated that after the kids went to their own homes, they had to call a neighbor first and tell them what they were doing before they visited. *Joe Dorociak*

CAN HUNT

Divide your entire group into teams and send them into the neighborhood for a limited time (30-45 minutes) to collect canned goods. The group with the most cans collected within the time limit wins a prize. It is amazing how many canned goods your kids can collect if the motivation is a contest. For some reason people respond more when they can help a young person win a contest than they do to help a starving family. *Larry Ballenger*

SCAVENGER FOOD HUNT

Develop a list of food items that will make up a complete meal. Divide your group into teams and go door-to-door attempting to get everything on the list. Each contributing family receives a small thank-you note explaining the purpose of the collection and where the food is going. The food can then be distributed to needy families. This scavenger hunt might be appropriate as a Halloween substitute for trick or treating. *Donald Durrett*

WORK-A-THON

Here's a service project that gets both kids and adults involved, plus helps fill needs at home and abroad. Have the kids in the youth group work for various people in the community who can't afford to pay for it or who are unable to do it themselves. This could include painting, gardening, housekeeping, shopping, or any other service that the kids could perform. Each kid gets one or more sponsoring adults to pay their wage—so much per hour—for each hour of work. The money collected—which can be a considerable amount—is given to feed hungry people in famine-stricken areas or to support missionaries in other lands. This way you get twice the mileage out of one act of service. *David Self*

GLEANING PARTY

If your community has public garden plots or is near farms, your group might consider the old system of gleaning—going through the fields after the harvest and salvaging all that is ripe and usable. The collected food is sorted and then given to an organization that distributes food to the poor. *Jim Couser*

KIDNAP THE PASTOR

Have a group kidnap the pastor or someone else well-known in the church—prearranged, of course. Set the ransom as canned goods (e.g., 100 cans) from the congregation to be used for distribution to needy families. This should be done on a Saturday. Kids then telephone people in the congregation informing them of the kidnapping and the ransom. The collection can be made on Sunday morning. If the ransom isn't paid up, the youths can be prepared to handle the morning service or the responsibilities of the kidnapped person. *Geoffrey Koglin*

SHUT-INS, THE SICK, THE HANDICAPPED

GET-WELL VIDEO

Is a member of your group in the hospital or facing a lengthy recuperation at home? Schedule an ice cream party in her honor and videotape the kids and adults who attend. Videotape students doing goofy things, and give everyone a chance to send messages via the tape. A small group of close friends can deliver the tape.

This easy, inexpensive, and entertaining project tells kids that you love them, you're praying for them, and you care. Adapt it to encourage those who are off to college and struggling with loneliness. *Mark A. Simone*

CHILDREN WITH SPECIAL NEEDS

Interacting with children who are retarded or have cerebral palsy, cystic fibrosis, MS, or leukemia can be a uniquely moving and growing opportunity for kids. Have the youth group plan an ongoing social activity for a group of such young people. Once a

month plan some kind of activity (swimming, movie, field trips, play, camping) and include food, refreshments, etc. Of course, there must be close cooperation with the clinic or agency from which the contact is made. Such activities would have to be prefaced by a series of introductory meetings with qualified workers who prepare your kids for the special do's and don'ts of working with that particular handicap. Some churches have formed ecumenical councils and rotate the monthly activities among different youth groups. *Dodd Lamberton*

VITAMIN BOXES

If someone in your youth group—or one of his friends—is confined for a long illness, have the other group members each bring an inexpensive,

wrapped gift to your next meeting. Place the gifts in a large box marked "Once-A-Day Vitamins." Deliver the box to the patient with instructions to open only one gift each day. The idea is to give him something to look forward to besides treatments. *Ralph Bryant*

ANIMAL BALLOONS

Pediatric patients at a nearby hospital—not to mention the hospital's public relations and floor staff—are usually enthusiastic about concrete acts of kindness extended to young patients.

Here's one gesture that your group can make. After you've obtained whatever permission you need from the hospital, make simple animal balloons—lions, monkeys, turtles—at home or church and distribute them personally among the juvenile patients. For the special balloons and instruction booklets you'll need, visit your local party supply shop or toy store. *Wayne Clause*

VISITATION LEADERS

To help your youth group have more meaningful visits to shut-ins, hospitals, and nursing homes, appoint one young person to each of the following four areas of responsibility:
- **Prayer.** Find volunteers for:
   —the opening prayer
   —the closing prayer
   —other prayer, if appropriate
- **Scripture.** Find someone to:
   —choose a passage
   —comment on it before reading it
   —state one point of the passage, after reading it, and discuss it
- **Music.** Locate people who will:
   —choose appropriate songs
   —take enough songbooks
   —find a musician(s)
   —perform some special music
- **Gifts.** One person should:
   —obtain appropriate gifts
   —obtain appropriate cards
   —have the cards signed and present the gifts and cards with a kind word on behalf of the group and the church

Daniel C. Broadwater

OFFICIAL PHOTOGRAPHER

If you have a young person in your group who is handicapped and unable to participate in some of the more active games, get her a Polaroid or other instant camera. Teach her how to use it properly and then make her the Official Youth Group Photographer. Whenever the youth group gets together, she takes pictures, and the kids always gather around her to see how the pictures turn out. This provides an otherwise neglected and left out young person a good opportunity to get lots of attention and to really feel needed and appreciated. The photos can be hung up on the youth group bulletin board. Be sure to use an instant camera—for obvious reasons. Otherwise the results are not the same. *Edie Owen*

ADOPT-A-GARDEN

Here's an idea that can really *grow* on you: Invite your group to adopt the gardens of shut-ins, chronically ill, hospitalized, or aged people. Supply the seeds and encourage youths to supply the tools and muscle power. They can prepare the soil, plant, cultivate, and ultimately harvest the crops, all for the people who own the gardens and are, of course, unable to do the work. It makes for great interaction between the generations. Especially helpful are youths who like farming, biology, or nature. Novices can learn fast too.

An adaptation of this idea involves others in the congregation. While publicizing Adopt-a-Garden, invite others who already have gardens to set aside one or two rows for giving away to the hungry. Again youths can supply the seeds and deliver the harvested produce to the needy. This can fit well into a long-range hunger-awareness program. *Jeremy Pera and Nate Castens*

SUMMER CAROLING

One method of bringing joy to people who are sick or shut-in is a summer caroling experience. Youths visit homes to sing songs and perhaps even prepare meals to eat with the residents. This activity can be incorporated into a slave day too, and work can be done for the needy. The minister might agree to join the youth group and administer communion in the homes of people unable to attend church. Cassette tapes and recorders can bring worship services and messages from friends to those who cannot leave their homes. *Denise Turner*

TREAT-MAKING PARTY

Have your youth group spend an evening making popcorn balls, fudge, cookies, and other treats. Then on a designated day—maybe Halloween—have them deliver the treats to an orphanage, hospital, or rest home. *Corinne Bergstom*

F.A.I.T.H. PROJECTS

Sometimes service projects come across as dreary duties with no connection to a personal faith in Christ. Why settle for mere service projects when you can offer F.A.I.T.H. projects: *F*aith *A*cting *I*n *T*eens' *H*ands. Tie every project directly to biblical faith and our responsibility to help others as representatives of Jesus.

With F.A.I.T.H. projects, teens find a new sense of confidence in their commitment to Christ as they learn to support others. Cleaning houses, mowing lawns, or washing cars takes on new meaning when they are seen as spiritual disciplines. Serving at social functions by waiting tables, washing dishes, or mopping floors become holy activities as kids see their hands as extensions of Jesus' hands.

Frightening tasks like working with the elderly or sick become easier when young people realize they are not alone with their challenge, but that God is at work through them. Adult responsibilities like the care of young children or the supervision of older children are seen as opportunities to learn patience under the influence of the Holy Spirit. These are also sacrificial acts that show Christlike mercy to parents who are relieved of their responsibilities for a time.

For an even more substantial sacrifice, use youth group funds to send those same parents out for the evening at a cozy restaurant and then to a bed-and-breakfast.

Challenge your group to be involved in F.A.I.T.H. projects on a regular basis—one every two months is realistic.

To get the most from F.A.I.T.H. projects, recruit leaders for this ministry rather than asking for volunteers. Some can be entirely youth led; other projects need adult supervision. Invest time in your leaders to help them understand the larger spiritual meaning of a project; then ask them to contact teens personally to serve. *Bryan Carpenter and Tommy Baker*

STUDENTS' BILL OF RIGHTS

Your students will be surprised what they *can* do as Christians on their school campuses when you distribute the bill of rights on page 87. *Tom Lytle*

V.I.S.I.O.N. TEAM

Need a name for your youth group volunteers? How about V.I.S.I.O.N. Team? It stands for *V*olunteers *I*nvesting *S*ome (Time) *I*n *O*thers' *N*eeds. Use Proverbs 29:18 as your motto: "Where there is no vision, the people perish." *KJV* *Bert and Cheryl Jones*

SERVANT CERTIFICATES

The certificates on page 89 are filled out by all the young people and presented to each other to be redeemed as noted. A lesson on Mark 10:42-45 makes an excellent introduction to this idea. *Bobby Guffey*

BIRTHDAY REMINDER

Your group can enlist the entire congregation to make your high school graduates feel special on their birthdays, even though they're away at college. Buy a bunch of 3x5 index cards, wet just a corner of first-class postage stamps, affix them to the index cards, write a catchy note on the cards,

This is a postage stamp!
You can—
A. Frame it and hang it on your doll-house wall.
B. Use it to repair the leak in your wading pool.
C. Stick it on the envelope of a birthday card to—
Kathy Smith
Box 100, All American College
anywhere, USA 00000
We'd be mighty grateful, of course, if you chose C. Kathy's birthday is May 3rd, by the way. Thanks!
—The youth group at First Church

STUDENTS' BILL OF RIGHTS ON A PUBLIC SCHOOL CAMPUS

I. THE RIGHT TO MEET WITH OTHER RELIGIOUS STUDENTS.
The Equal Access Act allows students the freedom to meet on campus for the purpose of discussing religious issues.

II. THE RIGHT TO IDENTIFY YOUR RELIGIOUS BELIEFS THROUGH SIGNS AND SYMBOLS.
Students are free to express their religious beliefs through signs and symbols.

III. THE RIGHT TO TALK ABOUT YOUR RELIGIOUS BELIEFS ON CAMPUS.
Freedom of speech is a fundamental right mandated in the Constitution and is not nullified in the school yard.

IV. THE RIGHT TO DISTRIBUTE RELIGIOUS LITERATURE ON CAMPUS.
Distributing literature on campus may not be restricted simply because the literature is religious.

V. THE RIGHT TO PRAY ON CAMPUS.
Students may pray alone or with others so long as it does not disrupt school activities or is not forced on others.

VI. THE RIGHT TO CARRY OR STUDY YOUR BIBLE ON CAMPUS.
The Supreme Court has said that only *state directed* Bible reading is unconstitutional.

VII. THE RIGHT TO DO RESEARCH PAPERS, SPEECHES, AND CREATIVE PROJECTS WITH RELIGIOUS THEMES.
The First Amendment does not forbid all mention of religion in public schools.

VIII. THE RIGHT TO BE EXEMPT.
Students may be exempt from activities and class contents that contradict their religious beliefs.

IX. THE RIGHT TO CELEBRATE OR STUDY RELIGIOUS HOLIDAYS ON CAMPUS.
Music, art, literature, and drama that have religious themes are permitted as part of the curriculum for school activities if presented in an objective manner as a traditional part of the cultural and religious heritage of the particular holiday.

X. THE RIGHT TO MEET WITH SCHOOL OFFICIALS.
The First Amendment to the Constitution forbids Congress to make any law that would restrict the right of the people to petition the Government (school officials).

Reprinted with permission. The complete book *Students' Legal Rights* is available by writing or calling Roever Communications, P.O. Box 136130, Fort Worth, TX 76136, phone 800/873-2839, www.interplaza.com/roever.

and then distribute them throughout your congregation.

Use the same idea for remembering kids at summer camp or on extended summer mission trips, or church members in the hospital. *Laura Shockley*

Armed Forces Social

This is a great way to minister to people in the service and/or college students away from home. The idea is to have a party fixing up packages to be sent to each of these people from your group or church. Parties could include baking cookies and making candy. Then package the goodies and mail them. You might also have the kids write a letter to each person—just a paragraph by each party attendee would make a great letter—and enclose a couple of photos of your group baking the cookies or playing games. For packing, use a plastic bag inside a coffee can, cut wrapping paper four inches longer on each end, then wrap and fold ends like coin wrappers. Now tie a string around them and knot. *Harold Antrim*

Towel Award

Here's a meaningful way to thank a youth group member who performs acts of service without seeking recognition. Present him or her with the Towel Award, a monogrammed towel set. This award should be given as a high honor and only to those

who have consistently performed acts of service without having been asked, and without calling attention to themselves.

The towel, a symbol of service in John 13, will remind everyone of the true meaning of servanthood. *Rick Brown*

Servant Certificate

The bearer of this certificate is hereby entitled to one unabashed, unheralded gift of service to be lovingly performed by me at your point of need and time of convenience. Just let me know!

To: _____

From: _____, your humble servant,

This _____ day of _____, 19_____.

(Mark 10:42-45)

Servant Certificate

The bearer of this certificate is hereby entitled to one unabashed, unheralded gift of service to be lovingly performed by me at your point of need and time of convenience. Just let me know!

To: _____

From: _____, your humble servant,

This _____ day of _____, 19_____.

(Mark 10:42-45)

YOUTH SPECIALTIES TITLES

Professional Resources

Administration, Publicity, & Fundraising (Ideas Library)

Developing Student Leaders

Equipped to Serve: Volunteer Youth Worker Training Course

Help! I'm a Junior High Youth Worker!

Help! I'm a Sunday School Teacher!

Help! I'm a Volunteer Youth Worker!

How to Expand Your Youth Ministry

How to Speak to Youth...and Keep Them Awake at the Same Time

One Kid at a Time: Reaching Youth through Mentoring

A Youth Ministry Crash Course

The Youth Worker's Handbook to Family Ministry

Youth Ministry Programming

Camps, Retreats, Missions, & Service Ideas (Ideas Library)

Compassionate Kids: Practical Ways to Involve Your Students in Mission and Service

Creative Bible Lessons in John: Encounters with Jesus

Creative Bible Lessons in Romans: Faith on Fire!

Creative Bible Lessons on the Life of Christ

Creative Junior High Programs from A to Z, Vol. 1 (A-M)

Creative Meetings, Bible Lessons, & Worship Ideas (Ideas Library)

Crowd Breakers & Mixers (Ideas Library)

Drama, Skits, & Sketches (Ideas Library)

Dramatic Pauses

Facing Your Future: Graduating Youth Group with a Faith That Lasts

Games (Ideas Library)

Games 2 (Ideas Library)

Great Fundraising Ideas for Youth Groups

Great Retreats for Youth Groups

Greatest Skits on Earth

Greatest Skits on Earth, Vol. 2

Holiday Ideas (Ideas Library)

Hot Illustrations for Youth Talks

Incredible Questionnaires for Youth Ministry

Junior High Game Nights

Kickstarters: 101 Ingenious Intros to Just about Any Bible Lesson

Memory Makers

More Great Fundraising Ideas for Youth Groups

More Hot Illustrations for Youth Talks

More Junior High Game Nights

Play It Again! More Great Games for Groups

Play It! Great Games for Groups

Special Events (Ideas Library)

Spontaneous Melodramas

Super Sketches for Youth Ministry

Teaching the Bible Creatively

Up Close and Personal: How to Build Community in Your Youth Group

Wild Truth Bible Lessons

Worship Services for Youth Groups

Discussion Starter Resources

Discussion & Lesson Starters (Ideas Library)

Discussion & Lesson Starters 2 (Ideas Library)

4th-6th Grade TalkSheets

Get 'Em Talking

High School TalkSheets

High School TalkSheets: Psalms and Proverbs

Junior High TalkSheets

Junior High TalkSheets: Psalms and Proverbs

Keep 'Em Talking!

More High School TalkSheets

More Junior High TalkSheets

What If...? 450 Thought-Provoking Questions to Get Teenagers Talking, Laughing, and Thinking

Would You Rather...? 465 Provocative Questions to Get Teenagers Talking

Clip Art

ArtSource Vol. 1—Fantastic Activities

ArtSource Vol. 2—Borders, Symbols, Holidays, and Attention Getters

ArtSource Vol. 3—Sports

ArtSource Vol. 4—Phrases and Verses

ArtSource Vol. 5—Amazing Oddities and Appalling Images

ArtSource Vol. 6—Spiritual Topics

ArtSource Vol. 7—Variety Pack

ArtSource Vol. 8—Stark Raving Clip Art

ArtSource CD-ROM (contains Vols. 1-7)

Videos

EdgeTV

The Heart of Youth Ministry: A Morning with Mike Yaconelli

Next Time I Fall in Love Video Curriculum

Understanding Your Teenager Video Curriculum

Student Books

Grow For It Journal

Grow For It Journal through the Scriptures

Wild Truth Journal for Junior Highers